P9-DHH-193

PRAISE FOR *BECOMING A CITIZEN ACTIVIST*

"Nick Licata is a rare combination of things: a thinker who knows grassroots activism, an idealist who can pragmatically wield power, and a politician who knows how to change culture. His compact book distills a career of great citizenship into simple lessons and memorable stories. I hope it inspires a new generation to become activists, in and out of office."

—ERIC LIU, founder and CEO of Citizen University

"Nick Licata knows that democracy isn't a spectator sport and that the voices of real people are needed to build the best nation possible. Through stories of successful campaigns, practical tips, and the sharing of hard-won lessons, this book guides the reader to become part of a democracy that works for everyone. An inspiring, must-read book for anyone who has ever dreamed of a better world."

—KRISTIN ROWE-FINKBEINER, executive director of MomsRising

"*Becoming a Citizen Activist* is a timely antidote to our poisoned democracy. At a time when corporations are treated as super-citizens while most individuals think of themselves only as taxpayers, Licata shares inspiring stories about the power of people and valuable advice for taking back our government."

—JIM DIERS, author of *Neighbor Power*

"*Becoming a Citizen Activist* is a wonderful compilation of specific anecdotes of successful social justice struggles led by ordinary people, practical tips for fighting for your cause, and compelling insights into power, politics, and the medley of strategies that make change happen."

—PRAMILA JAYAPAL, Washington state senator and founder of OneAmerica

"As someone who spent most of my adult life in elected office, it is refreshing to see someone from the 'inside' opening the playbook for those seeking civic change and social justice. Too many times we want the home run, when getting solid hits is the most effective way of enacting change. Sharing Nick Licata's wisdom is not likely to win friends within the halls of government, but I think it will help balance the scale for those working in the trenches."

—JIM HUNT, former president of the National League of Cities and founder of Amazing Cities

"*Becoming a Citizen Activist* provides inspiration and nuggets of practical advice for anyone who wants to fight city hall and build a better world."

—WENDY WENDLANDT, chair of the board of the Washington Public Interest Research Group

BECOMING A CITIZEN ACTIVIST

BECOMING A CITIZEN ACTIVIST

STORIES, STRATEGIES & ADVICE FOR CHANGING OUR WORLD

NICK LICATA

SASQUATCH BOOKS
SEATTLE

Copyright © 2016 by Nick Licata

All rights reserved. No portion of this book may
be reproduced or utilized in any form, or by any
electronic, mechanical, or other means, without the
prior written permission of the publisher.

Printed in the United States of America

Published by Sasquatch Books

20 19 18 17 16   9 8 7 6 5 4 3 2 1

Editor: Gary Luke
Production editor: Em Gale
Design and lettering: Joyce Hwang
Copyeditor: Janice Lee
Photographs: © Dan Lamont / author photo
© Kritchanut/ Dreamstime/ Starburst 34444560

Library of Congress Cataloging-in-Publication
Data is available.

ISBN: 978-1-63217-044-6

Sasquatch Books
1904 Third Avenue, Suite 710
Seattle, WA 98101
(206) 467-4300
www.sasquatchbooks.com
custserv@sasquatchbooks.com

Certified Chain of Custody
SUSTAINABLE   Promoting Sustainable Forestry
FORESTRY
INITIATIVE   www.sfiprogram.org
              SFI-01268

SFI label applies to the text stock

This book is dedicated to those working to sustain a democracy that allows its citizens the freedom to shape their future, free of prejudice and poverty

CONTENTS

ACKNOWLEDGMENTS

I thank the following people for assisting me:

My daughter, Eleanor Licata, for reviewing endless drafts with a gentle but firm editorial touch.

My ever-vigilant crew of Lisa Herbold, Newell Aldrich, and Frank Video for keeping me honest most of the time.

My literary agent, Anne Depue, who provided me encouragement and invaluable guidance.

My editor and publisher, Gary Luke, who believed that I could convince others to change the world.

And my wife, Andrea Okomski, for her much-appreciated steadfast support.

PROLOGUE

You don't have to be a Marvel comic book superhero to change the world. You don't even have to be a saint, a revolutionary, a political leader, or a community organizer. You just have to be aware of your surroundings and of the opportunities to improve your life and those of others.

Certainly if you are driven to improve the world, this book should help you evaluate various strategies and tactics to employ. I reference what I've learned from my experience and that of others. It will hopefully help you go from wanting change to initiating change. The lessons that follow should help you minimize the risk of failure and maximize success in taking on that effort.

However, the theme here is that every citizen should have the power to meaningfully participate in a democracy. Too often citizens defer to politicians, as if they are the only ones who should exercise power. You don't need to start a movement to challenge the status quo, but you do have the power to question it.

Ultimately, change begins with you. You have to help yourself create your own future. If you don't, someone else will.

CHAPTER 1
YOU CAN FIGHT CITY HALL

The Minimum Wage Story

The first step to becoming an active citizen is to find out who has power, knock on their door, and say open it up. If the door doesn't open, then you have a choice: you can walk away or have the courage to knock harder until they open the door.

Martina Phelps and Jason Harvey, workers at fast-food franchises in Seattle, found that courage when they walked out on their jobs to protest their low salaries and poor working conditions. The lowest-paid workers, the citizens with the least amount of power, began the struggle that led to a victory that echoed around the nation. On June 2, 2014, the Seattle City

Council unanimously (9–0) passed a law increasing the minimum wage to fifteen dollars an hour in the city, making it the highest minimum wage in the nation at that time. They did so only after citizens like Phelps and Harvey organized and made that demand.

Phelps was twenty-one when she began working at a McDonald's. After eight months of working there, she noticed that her paycheck was not reflecting the hours she worked. It was a classic case of wage theft; the employer was not paying a worker for hours served. She repeatedly complained to her supervisors. They ignored her. She talked to her fellow workers; they too had similar experiences, and their complaints had been ignored. It got so bad that she realized that she had to take it upon herself. "I just didn't care what they thought of me. They were not part of my family. No one cared, and I had to do what was necessary to do."

She and four of her fellow employees participated in a national one-day walkout in May 2013 to protest their disrespectful treatment, their unpaid wages, and their low hourly wages. She said that after the walkout, her supervisors treated her even worse. "The corporation came down heavy, and the managers were watching us more closely than ever before; they tried to scare everyone. One of the workers was harassed so badly that he just quit his job." However, she kept working and continued to speak up at public hearings and rallies, letting the public know how bad the working conditions were at fast-food franchises.

Jason Harvey was thirty-six years old when he began working at Burger King. After working for them for eight years, he was still making the state minimum wage. The same was true for the other workers at his Burger King and the other thirty Burger King stores that the franchise owner controlled in the Puget Sound region. A few people did ask the manager for raises. The manager said that they did get one every year, when their salary was adjusted upward by the yearly state-mandated standard-of-living increase. Since that amounted to wages that just kept their heads above the water, many employees quit to look for better-paying work.

The fast-food industry has a notoriously high turnover, yet many folks cannot elevate themselves out of those jobs, because better work options don't exist for them. More Starbucks baristas than you would expect are underemployed college graduates. As Harvey said, "People come and go all the time." The employees at Harvey's Burger King were not high school youth leaving for college; most were in their thirties. Across the nation, the average minimum wage worker is thirty-five years old. Over a quarter are parents, like two women who worked with Harvey, one in her fifties and the other in her sixties.

Harvey heard one day that the fast-food industry was lobbying the state legislature to create a new training-wage category below the state minimum wage. He was already under pressure to reduce his hours, and if the legislation passed, even lower-paid employees working as trainees could pick up his lost hours. Around that time, Harvey met Clay Dewey-Valentine, who stopped by the Burger King and told him about Working Washington, a coalition of various neighborhood and religious groups backed by organized labor. Harvey liked what he heard and invited Dewey-Valentine over to his apartment to continue their discussion on what was happening in the state legislature. He didn't want to be seen talking to someone about workers' rights at Burger King. He was aware that organizing got results. He saw how the city council passed a law mandating paid sick leave for all employees, and that was due to a very public organizing campaign. He was grateful for the new law, since before then he had no such coverage, and used it to take a day off when he was sick.

Harvey took a significant step; he signed an initiative to oppose the training wage in Olympia. Later he attended a meeting of Working Washington and was told about a planned national strike of fast-food workers to push for higher wages. He thought and prayed about whether he should participate. He couldn't discuss it with many of his co-workers because he didn't speak Spanish and most of them didn't speak English. It was a frightening decision to make. "Part of me was scared out of my wits to do something like this, as necessary as it was to do. But courage is not the absence of fear; it's telling fear what its place is." When the time came for the one-day walkout, Harvey walked out of his job, alone, although at other stores, many more went on strike.

Afterward employees at Harvey's store were emboldened, but management kept them in line by firing some, although

Harvey kept his job. The owner promoted a few to assistant manager, where they would earn thirty cents more an hour but could not go on strike for higher wages because they were considered management. Harvey continued to work there and even addressed the city council at a public hearing. He said, "If you don't do what you have to do to make things better, they'll just get worse."

When the fast-food workers' walkout began asking for a minimum wage of fifteen dollars an hour, politicians like me (serving as a Seattle city councilmember) were sympathetic but also felt that fifteen dollars was way too big of a lift. In my own case, I thought there were more readily achievable goals, like fighting wage theft. I found myself initially offering cautious verbal support and not much more.

Luckily Phelps, Harvey, and other fast-food workers had a powerful and determined ally in David Rolf, president of the Service Employees International Union (SEIU) 775, who was the driving force behind the efforts of SEIU and other organizations to raise the minimum wage to fifteen dollars in the city of SeaTac. That measure was on the November 2013 ballot. SeaTac has a population of twenty-seven thousand, and the measure would raise the wages of six thousand employees working at large transportation and hospitality businesses in and around Seattle-Tacoma International Airport just south of Seattle. For the first time, the fifteen-dollar minimum wage would be tested at the ballot. Hoping to rally the public behind an economic justice proposal, SEIU devoted full-time staff and financial resources to mobilize volunteers and to educate the public about the necessity of improving the lives of the poorest and most exploited workers in their community.

Even before SeaTac's vote, the struggle for the fifteen-dollar minimum wage was an active issue in Seattle. Instead of six thousand workers, one hundred thousand would benefit from having a fifteen-dollar minimum wage in Seattle, according to a University of Washington study. In May 2013, Phelps, Harvey, and others walked out on their jobs and brought the struggle for a just minimum wage to Seattle.

Elections Count

When pushing for monumental change, like significantly raising the minimum wage, it is necessary to have politicians willing to back those demands. Most will shy away from taking on what would seem to be an insurmountable task. So when one or two step up and champion the issue, you must support their election campaigns with contributions and volunteer hours if your cause is to be taken seriously. This may even require abandoning public officials who have been sympathetic in the past but have different views on this most critical issue.

By chance, when the fast-food walkouts occurred, Seattle was in the midst of local elections for mayor and city council candidates. State senator Ed Murray was challenging the incumbent mayor, Mike McGinn. Both were liberals. McGinn had headed up the regional Sierra Club, and Murray had attracted national attention for being one of the few gay politicians to successfully get his state to legalize gay marriage. There were also four incumbent city councilmembers, including me, running for reelection to citywide positions. Most of the attention was focused on the mayor's race, since none of the council incumbents appeared to have serious challengers. Then something happened.

In addition to Phelps and Harvey, many other Seattle residents working in similar jobs were aware of how poor their working conditions were. The cost of living in Seattle was so high that even when they were working full time at minimum wage, 60 percent of their annual gross salary would be needed to pay for an average rental. Even those earning more could see how their friends could barely make their rent or mortgage payments or pay their health-care bills.

The first and boldest candidate to support raising the minimum wage to fifteen dollars an hour was a seemingly minor candidate for city council, Kshama Sawant. She was an immigrant from India, a community college professor in economics, and a leader in the Socialist Alternative Party. Her statements would not have made much of a difference. There had been socialist candidates running for city council for years. Most had been ignored by the media and rarely made it past the primary.

However, there was a major difference that distinguished her campaign from the others. She understood that organizing is more than chanting slogans; it is working one-on-one with people to convince them there's something to believe in.

She ran against Richard Conlin, a sixteen-year incumbent, who had built a solid reputation promoting sustainability issues like local farmers' markets and transit rail lines. Although he strongly supported funding human-service agencies, he was the lone vote against the council's paid sick leave legislation. When Sawant announced her campaign for his seat, it created as much stir in the established political circles as another drop of rain in Seattle. Conlin ignored her and the growing cry for raising the minimum wage. In turn, many who had supported him turned their attention to Sawant.

As an activist you can echo the anger and hopes of the disenfranchised. But to make institutional changes, you need an organization that can mobilize people to join together to support and work for an issue or candidate. The Democratic and Republican Parties have largely monopolized that role. Occasionally third-party efforts break through to get one of their own elected to office. More often an outsider from one of those two establishment parties or a candidate who creates his or her own party receives a significant electoral vote through personally financing a campaign. Think of Ross Perot, who spent $100 million (in 2010 dollars) to run for president in 1992, or Michael Bloomberg, who spent $73 million to win New York City's 2001 mayoral election.

Sawant was not rich, but she did have a small political party, Socialist Alternative, which was started in the late eighties. At the time she ran, twenty major cities had chapters. While proudly socialist, the party was pragmatic enough to support Ralph Nader's independent presidential campaigns.

Although they had few members in Seattle and limited financial resources, they demonstrated the power of a small, organized group armed with a message that resonated with the public. Much like the Occupy movement, it was a revolt of the 99 percent who were missing out on America's prosperity. In Seattle, it consisted of students, workers, the unemployed, and people of all political persuasions who did not like to see the nation's growing income inequality.

When you win over one politician, don't stop there. Keep pushing others to take a position; there is no better time to do so than when they are running for office. The race for mayor was growing tight, and the challenger, state senator Ed Murray, recognized that raising the minimum wage was an important issue and the right thing to do. With six weeks before people would start voting, he endorsed a fifteen-dollar minimum wage. It was no longer just a socialist pipe dream. A well-established politician was now saying let's do it. Even with caveats that it should be phased in and targeted at "fast-food brands and big-box retail" stores, it was a bold statement. Suddenly, a fifteen-dollar minimum wage seemed politically possible.

The incumbent mayor, Mike McGinn, although very pro-labor, missed opportunities to clearly state that he would introduce the fifteen-dollar minimum wage in Seattle by suggesting that the state might be better positioned to make this change. Meanwhile, Councilmember Richard Conlin was videotaped by the Sawant campaign telling an audience, "I don't support the fifteen-dollar minimum wage." He offered to study it if reelected. It was a moment of truth for many of McGinn's and Conlin's supporters: should they stick with old friends who were talking of studies or suggesting that the state should act instead of the city, or go with the new candidates who were more clearly committed to moving the city forward with this change?

It was a classic example of a politician not seizing the moment, not being aware of how strong the public sentiment was on this issue. On Election Day, Murray became mayor and Sawant became the first socialist elected to Seattle's local government in over a hundred years, defeating a well-liked liberal politician. What happened?

You need more than the right message to win a struggle; you need to be organized. You need to mobilize those who have the most to gain and have been ignored by others.

It was not at all apparent that Sawant could win the general election after she got past the primary. However, in the month before the general election, her volunteer base had swollen with many disaffected Democrats who wanted more aggressive councilmembers willing to speak out on issues. Identifying who would respond to her message was key to Sawant's victory. On election night Conlin conceded that his opponent had "clearly tapped into some interest that people have."

How strongly she tapped that interest grew more evident as the vote tally changed following the first returns. Seattle voters receive their ballots approximately twenty days before the election and can mail them in as late as Election Day. Each day, as more votes were counted, the gap narrowed.

Sawant's campaign targeted occasional and new voters. It is typical in nonpresidential election years to go after the "perfect voters," who vote in every election. Generally they are seniors and homeowners, not younger people entering the job market and those who cannot afford to buy a home. Sawant's call for a fifteen-dollar minimum wage caught the attention of people tired of being stuck in low-paying jobs, unable to move out of cramped apartments. They were aware that they had to do something to improve their lives.

The elections themselves did not guarantee that there would be a fifteen-dollar minimum wage. Many elections have been won on slogans that were never realized. To actually achieve a goal, you have to consider how to use the political power of government and the social power of the populace to push for change. I'll cover those strategies later in the book, but first I'll describe how seeing, listening, learning, and organizing are all critical steps to becoming an effective, active citizen— one who can make our democracy responsive and accountable. Achieving a fifteen-dollar minimum wage in Seattle is just one example of how those skills can come together to change the world.

CHAPTER 2
SEE THE WORLD AS IT SHOULD BE

We see the world as we are taught to see it. Over time we may notice that some things don't match what we were taught. We might ignore the difference or think that we saw it wrong. But sometimes we see that things actually are wrong.

I was taught to see the world as an orderly arrangement of responsibilities. I was responsible to my parents. My dad was responsible to his boss. Time and again he advised me, "Do as your boss tells you." We were all responsible to our church, the Roman Catholic Church. I took catechism classes throughout high school, so I could carefully measure the number of venial and mortal sins I had accumulated before confessing them and starting over again, resolved to have fewer before my next confession. It was an orderly world.

The first time I remember seeing something that didn't match what I had been taught was in third grade while I was standing in the Saint Patrick Elementary School's playground in Cleveland during recess. There was a game called "pile on." The rules were simple. A group of boys, generally the bigger ones, would run around the schoolyard and choose some kid who didn't fit in, being either too fat, too skinny, or just too odd looking. Then they would pile onto him, literally smothering him with their bodies. It just didn't look right to me. I asked a nun patrolling the yard to intervene. She advised me to mind my own business and walked away. I learned then that those in authority don't always look out for the weakest despite what they tell us.

Read beyond the Words

It helps to have someone show you how to learn to look at the world differently. We are social creatures, and those we socialize with influence our views. If your friends passively accept what those in authority hand down, chances are that you will too. But if you have friends who prod those making the decisions, listen closely to what they are asking, because their questions could represent your concerns as well.

For me, that someone was Ivan, a fellow student at Bowling Green State University in Ohio whom I met one evening in a coffeehouse at closing time. We were the last two there, both writing bad poetry at separate tables. Ivan walked over and introduced himself. He had a Teddy Roosevelt grin while talking, and like TR, he wore small wire-frame glasses. He was about my height but stouter, with a barrel chest and an upright chin on his pimpled face.

Early in our conversation he asked if I was a Roman Catholic. I said yes, and he admitted he was too. That evening Ivan, with a few quips, like arrows piercing helium balloons, popped the infallibility of the Church, the logic of the university's rules, and my certainty that I would forever live in Cleveland. I laughed and, encouraged, he continued popping other balloons. He was a one-man precursor to *Saturday Night Live*. Moreover, everything he said struck me as having a note of truth. My grip around some firmly held beliefs began to loosen. I understand how humor can be the sharpest blade for cutting the cords that bind us to tradition. Humorists are the most dangerous of subversives in questioning the legitimacy of accepting things as they are.

One day we were walking across the campus. Ivan, reading our college newspaper, the *BG News*, suddenly stopped and slapped the back of his hand against the paper. "They're changing from the semester system to the quarter system." It was a small article tucked away in the inside pages. But it caught his eye. He was seeing something that I didn't. I too had skimmed over the piece. My response was passive. I viewed it as something that was happening to us.

Ivan, on the other hand, saw something different. "They didn't ask us. We're the ones being affected." It hadn't occurred to me that we should be asked or even that we had the right to be asked. With his sharp comment, I could see something I hadn't seen before. I realized that I had to do more than just read words; I had to peel them back to reveal what they were conveying. I had to realize how the information I read was shaping how I saw the world. And finally, if I cared, I had to ask myself if I would do something about it.

"We should do something," I said, not thinking of anything in particular. "We'll start a petition," Ivan said without pausing.

I had never signed a petition, let alone started one. But I liked the idea. Here was a chance to do something on campus that went beyond the confines of the classroom and that was more relevant than getting drunk and partying. As the first of my family to graduate from high school, not to mention go to college, I was looking forward to an exciting world filled with discussions about interesting topics. Instead I mostly found boring teachers and disinterested students. There was very little excitement, with the exception of drunken students yelling outside our dorm room late at night on the way back from one of the town's few bars.

We wrote a short statement urging the board of trustees to retain the semester system until they consulted with the students. Next we faced the problem of reproducing our request. There were no photocopiers or Internet connections in the sixties, and using a printing press would have been too expensive. But there was the mimeograph, a work-horse mechanical wonder that allowed one to cut a stencil on treated paper and then run off a limited number of reprints. It lives only in boomers' memories. The various university fraternities, social associations, and departments controlled most of the mimeographs. We had no connection to these institutions. But we did discover a subculture of artists and writers congregating in the Crypt, a faux coffeehouse in the basement of the United Christian Fellowship Center.

On the weekends, the Crypt served coffee and doughnuts, and had an open mic for students strumming guitars. It played a critical role in allowing students to mingle and exchange thoughts on everything from the arts to politics. I began to realize how informal gathering places, be they coffeehouses or taverns, could serve as boiling pots for open debate and incubators for troublemakers challenging established powers. The Protestant minister running the center was generous with his mimeograph; perhaps he enjoyed creating a little intellectual mischief by allowing his guests to circulate their grievances on campus.

The day after the article on the quarter system ran, Ivan and I stood in the middle of the campus quad casually stopping students between classes and asking them to sign our petition. Some had never seen a petition before and avoided us; others thought they might get in trouble if they signed. Some were cynical and thought any objections to university practices were futile. And some, doubtful of our effort, signed it anyway.

By the end of the day, we had almost two hundred signatures. The following day, a *BG News* reporter showed up, took our photo, and interviewed us while we gathered more signatures. Two days after we had begun our effort, I woke to see ourselves on the paper's front page. I was quoted: "We want this to be a measure of the students' concern with both the new system and the tactics used to initiate it."

I was surprised by the attention our one-page petition received, with no organization behind it, no committee meetings to discuss it, and no one in authority to approve it. We simply stopped and asked students their views, and it got us front-page coverage. Getting the university to relinquish power was another thing. Although our actions did not stop the conversion, I saw how carefully reading what we come across every day offers an opportunity to ask who is making the decisions that are affecting our lives and whether we care about those decisions. And if we do care, we should ask why those decisions were made and how we can become part of the decision-making process.

See the Small Things That Generate the Big Things

In looking around our urban landscape, we need to consider how seemingly innocuous practices shape our physical environment. Consider the use of plastic bags. They were relatively rare until the early nineties, when new engineering lowered their cost to about a cent per bag in the United States, less than a fourth of the cost of paper bags. In 2003, Robert Bateman, president of Roplast Industries, a manufacturer of plastic bags, said, "The plastic bags are so inexpensive that in the stores no one treats them as worth anything. . . . They use two, three, or four when one would do just as well." Consequently, the United States International Trade Commission reported in 2009 that 102 billion plastic bags were being used annually in the United States.

Like most people, I used them all the time. And like others, I did not see how they choked marine life, littered our landscape, and added to our demand for oil. They have also caused massive devastation, as Bangladesh discovered in 1998 when two-thirds of the nation was flooded, making thirty million people homeless. After discovering that large buildups of plastic bags had clogged their drainage systems, Bangladesh banned them in 2002. That same year Ireland began to charge a fee for using them, resulting in a 94 percent drop in plastic bag usage. Ireland's strategy inspired a number of California cities to charge a fee for plastic bags at checkout, and Seattle was to follow.

In Seattle activists were aware of this problem, but what was missing was a triggering event to mobilize public opinion. If you are working on an issue that needs to be addressed but does not have a sense of immediacy, like the gradual proliferation of plastic bags, look for an incident that will highlight the impact that it has on our environment and our lives.

That opportunity to mobilize public opinion, beyond the small but organized environmental community concerned with this issue, was provided in 2007 when the City of Seattle proposed building a new waste-transfer station in its Georgetown neighborhood. The anticipated increase in truck and rail traffic to move the waste to landfills rallied the residents to oppose the City's plans. At the public hearings, residents began to question the City's entire strategy for waste removal. Holly Krejci, one of Georgetown's resident leaders, explained to me, "We began to ask, why are we sending out mile-long trains filled with trash? Why not just reduce waste?" She and her partner, fellow community leader Kathy Nyland, met with Councilmember Richard Conlin to encourage him to take this path. "He was very pleased that citizens were pursuing this strategy, since he needed popular support to convince city bureaucrats that this was the right thing to do," Nyland said.

Politicians often know what the right thing to do is, but unless there is an organized constituency to put pressure on other public officials, they may feel they don't have enough support to get legislation passed. The role of a citizen activist is to coax politicians to have the courage to pursue their own beliefs.

Citizen-initiated strategies need organizations and their leaders to grab the attention of city hall. Heather Trim was one of those leaders in Seattle's waste reduction movement. She had been working with an environmental group when she received a phone call from a woman wanting to get rid of Styrofoam packaging. Trim was already aware of plastic bags' impact on marine life and thought, why not also eliminate Styrofoam packaging? She then formed the volunteer group Zero Waste Seattle, which became the lead organization lobbying city council to eliminate both plastic bags and Styrofoam containers.

Conlin, now knowing he had strong community support, came out with his Zero Waste Strategy, which effectively derailed the need for a new transfer station in the city. He later explained that his approach was to focus on waste reduction as the next step beyond recycling. "We put this out for a public hearing, and we had hundreds of people show up, and basically nobody opposed it," he said.

City staff initially saw it as too expensive and resisted the change. While activists focus much energy on elected officials, often the decision making is greatly influenced by staff who public officials rely upon for detailed analysis. To counter bad information provided by government staff, it is necessary to have an organization that can provide outside data. In this instance established environmental organizations, like the Sierra Club, provided it. With their help, the citizens persuaded the mayor and the council to adopt a new waste reduction and recycling strategy in 2007. Among other things, the strategy banned foam containers and required a twenty-cent "green fee" on all disposable shopping bags. The city council passed it in July 2008 with only one dissenting vote.

The plastic bag industry financed a referendum to force a pub-lic vote on Conlin's legislation. After paying $180,000 to hire people to gather the necessary number of signatures to require a public vote, the industry spent another $1.4 million to over-turn the law. They won by a vote of 53 percent to 47 percent. Although the referendum had eliminated the plastic bag fee, the Styrofoam container ban remained in force and became one of the first and strongest in the nation.

Meanwhile the plastic bag disposal problem continued to grow. The city's daily newspaper, the *Seattle Times*, reported in 2010 that a beached gray whale was found to have twenty plastic bags in its stomach! Seattle Public Utilities found that PCB levels in Chinook salmon from Puget Sound were three to five times higher than in any other West Coast populations.

While it was not possible to see the mass of approximately 292 million plastic bags used annually in the city, citizens could see their impact and continued to ask the city coun-cil to do something about it. Newly elected councilmember Mike O'Brien worked for months with conservation groups to write legislation that would ban rather than tax plastic bags. The path to their success was dependent on address-ing the concerns of two significant groups who could oppose the legislation: the business community and the low-income minority community. They were able to convince part of the business community to support the ban. The Northwest Grocery Association, which represented QFC, Safeway, and Fred Meyer stores in the state, agreed to the ban in exchange for the right to implement a five-cent charge on paper bags made of at least 40 percent recycled paper. Next O'Brien wrote the legislation so that low-income people who could show proof of eligibility in a food-assistance program would not be charged the paper bag fee.

On December 19, 2011, the Seattle City Council passed a broad ban on plastic bags, and the plastic industry did not challenge the ban in the courts or at the polls. The following year, Los Angeles joined forty-seven other California cities and counties in adopting a ban on single-use plastic bags at retail checkouts, making it the largest US city to phase out the single-use bags. In the spring of 2014, the Chicago City Council also passed a plastic bag ban.

The phenomenal success of the plastic-ban movement reveals how citizens can set major societal changes in motion within a short period of time. In a span of just seven years, the number of US cities and counties banning or taxing plastic bags and Styrofoam containers went from practically zero to 132 cities and counties with a population of more than twenty million. And it all started with citizens seeing what politicians did not.

CHAPTER 3
LEARN TO LISTEN

The Politics of Anger

I have found that if you go out of your way to listen to those who you most strongly disagree with, you can gain insights on how they are successful in reaching people you want to reach. In learning what they say and how they say it, you can learn how to reach those same people with your message.

In the 1968 presidential election, civil rights were a significant issue. However, while the far left was fractured, running multiple candidates, the far right was coalescing around one man, former Alabama governor George Wallace. Although he had been a Democrat, he ran as an independent candidate and as the nation's foremost advocate for racial segregation. He had personally barred the path of two black students attempting to register at the University of Alabama in 1963. But he was also seen as a populist, supporting increased social security and Medicare benefits, while attacking hippies for not working and liberals for being soft on crime.

In the spring of my junior year of college, I heard that Wallace was going to give a campaign speech in Toledo, Ohio, less than a half hour from the town of Bowling Green. I talked a few friends into joining me at his rally. I did not go to protest; that would have been futile, given the audience's orientation. Instead, I wanted to understand what Wallace's attraction was and to see how he interacted with his audience. Not only would I then better understand his arguments, but I would also see how he delivered his message.

We walked into a packed Toledo high school gym; the bleachers were filled with working-class people. We found ourselves sitting high above the podium with a perfect bird's-eye view of the audience. These were familiar folks—the kind I had grown up with. Not a suit or tie among them. The men sported trim haircuts and neat casual clothing. The women were dressed modestly: no short skirts or jeans. This was not a college-age crowd.

I thought their ordinary attire belied a simmering rage within them. The crowd stamped their feet like a marching band in anticipation of Wallace's arrival. It grew louder with time. They had more passion than I had witnessed at antiwar rallies.

When Wallace finally appeared, everyone rose and clapped with a mighty roar. As if he were a maestro in front of an orchestra, he stepped up to the podium and proceeded to whip them into an ever-higher pitch of anger at everything that was wrong with this country, from pampered college students rioting in the streets to black welfare dads refusing to work. Women nodded and men shouted in agreement when Wallace said that rich liberal elites controlled both the Democratic and Republican Parties. He repeated his famous line, "There's not a dime's worth of difference between the Democrat and Republican Parties." I had heard that sentiment at home and, somewhat ironically, at antiwar rallies. He had touched on a widely shared belief: citizens had no control over their own government.

Looking down, I noticed a dozen black students stood on the main floor right below Wallace's podium, vociferously objecting to his racist remarks. Wallace snarled and pointed to them, as if they were ready-made props to focus the white crowd's hate. United against a common enemy, the audience catapulted insults down onto them. I feared for their safety, but they weren't physically harmed. Wallace needed them as a foil, not as victims.

Although neither a handsome Kennedy nor an erudite McCarthy, Wallace cut a swath through the Democrats' core of blue-collar voters. That evening I felt the heat of their resentment toward those who didn't have to work as hard as they did to make a living. Wallace would jab his finger at the audience, as if poking them, and point out that black people, college students, and liberals were receiving benefits that they would never receive. He was a master at reading the crowd and reflecting their anger. His ability reminded me of something Leon Trotsky wrote: "An unexcelled ability to detect the mood of the masses was Lenin's great power." Apparently it is an ability unencumbered by ideology. Even though Wallace did not win, his message had resonated with working families—the very ones that the left was trying to attract.

Driving back to Bowling Green, I thought of the Reverend Martin Luther King Jr.'s speech that I had heard in New York City the previous year. King spoke with indignation rather than raw anger and with hope rather than envy, appealing to reason and even love. Wallace was a demagogue who unleashed tremendous energy from the dark side of the collective soul. There would be no compromising for him; there was either victory or defeat. This was an attitude that unfortunately began to grow in 1968 on the far left as well. Except in that case, it was either revolution now or failure.

I came away from the Wallace rally seeing how appealing to the built-up anger in people and blaming those who are weaker, like the black students, or those who are far off, like the politicians in DC, could generate excitement and a sense of purpose. But it did not build bridges between people, which I felt was the basis of a democracy that could sustain rational change to benefit all. Democracy is the great leveler, but it only works if people believe that they have power as citizens. I came away believing that being an activist is not about promoting absolute solutions, which stirs passions while obstructing logic; it's about addressing people's anger by giving them some control over their lives.

Let the Police Speak

Over a long period of time in many cities, the media has reported incidents of police using excessive force on minority groups, particularly blacks and Latinos, for minor infractions. Citizen activists wanting to develop respectful relations between the police force and all citizens often demand accountability through demonstrations and petitioning. If successful, they achieve it through greater regulatory oversight of the police officers. In Seattle, activists were also open to listening to the concerns of the police officers in order to see if there was any common ground they could mutually address without giving up demands for police accountability. If you want to change the behavior of others, you may need to acknowledge that they have some valid concerns. The easiest way to find out is to ask them.

The city council created a civilian-led oversight body of police conduct in 1999, the Office of Professional Accountability (OPA). Attached to it was a civilian review board, which was allowed to see the names of officers who had complaints filed against them. However, the Seattle Police Officers' Guild (SPOG) challenged this transparency and managed to have police officers' names redacted, making it difficult for the review board to determine patterns of complaints against individual officers. The need for this information was evident when an OPA review of use-of-force complaints from 2003 to

2005 revealed that "a high proportion of complaints about force [were] made by citizens of color."

Whenever new information is brought forward that supports your position, do not let it sit idle. Use it. In this case citizens used the report the year it came out to pressure the city council to restore the citizen review board's access to the names of police officers with complaints filed against them. And when SPOG filed an appeal, citizens pushed the council to fight it in the courts. If the legislative branch fails, use their support to carry the struggle into the next branch of government, the judicial system.

In 2007, the City won back the right to view police officers' names. The following year the OPA auditor wrote a report examining patterns related to arrests of citizens being charged with obstructing officers from performing their duties. It found that among the seventy-six "obstruction only" charges reviewed, 51 percent involved black individuals, even though they account for less than 9 percent of Seattle's population. The police culture needed to change, and citizen oversight was exposing it but not necessarily changing it. When I met with activists, we agreed that we needed to start a dialogue with the police officers. But how?

I learned that the City's electric utility department had conducted an employee survey about their work conditions and thought a similar one should be offered to police officers. I approached the police chief, but he was reluctant, dismissing the idea as one that would probably just result in nothing new—officers always complain about a police chief and his staff. I then made my pitch to the SPOG leadership, asking if police officers had taken a survey in the past. They hadn't, and SPOG welcomed the opportunity, provided that they had input and distributed it.

I brought their response to citizens monitoring police conduct, and they felt that the major focus should be on the controversial issue of civilian oversight of the police. How did the police feel about it, and how could it work better for them? We made it clear to the officers that the survey was not about eliminating the OPA. With SPOG as an unexpected alley, the chief relented.

Citizen activists had outmaneuvered the City's bureaucracy by uniting on a common plan of action with their opponents. Citizens often find that the biggest obstacle to change is government inertia. It is difficult to wrestle with, because its reluctance is couched in soft general terms and processes. But government hesitation will often melt away if opposing parties agree to a common course of action. That is why it is important to talk to your opponents. You need to think of how to work with them to overcome a common antagonist; often it is an unresponsive government.

The council hired two academics to design and administer the survey. The findings, released in 2007, showed that a majority of officers investigated felt they were treated with respect, their rights were protected, the investigation was thorough, and the findings were fair. These perceptions were not what SPOG had been representing, so it helped citizens directly respond to SPOG's objections to civilian oversight.

In addition, a number of improvements were suggested, two of which coincided with those made by civilians. Both wanted investigations to be completed in a timely manner, so the council hired an extra investigator and most cases were closed within ninety days. In addition, over two-thirds of the officers as well as many citizens complained of not receiving investigative updates or the ultimate disposition of cases. In response the council provided investigators with additional training to enhance interview and research skills, and to teach the importance of regular status updates during the course of an investigation for officers and citizens alike.

The survey also showed that officers supported mediation efforts, and those who used mediation showed high satisfaction rates. In response the council funded mediation procedures, particularly with regard to complaints of rude conduct, the third-largest source of complaints reported by citizens.

After these changes were adopted, the satisfaction level of both officers and citizens dealing with the OPA increased. However, serious problems continued to arise regarding use of force, to the extent that the Department of Justice placed the City under a consent decree in 2012 to address this and other issues.

Fair and accountable law enforcement is one of the major problems that citizens will continue to face, because we are a socially dynamic, multiethnic nation. Consequently there will always be a need for citizen oversight of police departments. To be an effective activist in that process, it is important to listen to police officers and find common solutions to promote transparent procedures, reliable data collection, and mutual respect.

Women Reshape Local Government

Don't be afraid to be part of the system if you know what you want. In the late sixties the women's movement was gaining steam nationally as women across the nation were pushing for Congress to pass the Equal Rights Amendment. While the national women's movement was mobilizing to change federal laws, many women activists also saw that progress could be made at the local level. A significant step—and a necessary one—is getting someone elected who is going to champion your issue.

Jeanette Williams, a Seattle city council candidate in 1969, ran on a platform of social accountability to citizens, particularly to women and working people. She had been a leader in the labor movement at a time when men dominated the field. She ran for an open seat with her main opponent being another woman who had been endorsed by both daily newspapers and a civic activist group interested in reform. But Williams distinguished herself by strongly campaigning for the interests of all women.

After she won, it would have been easy for women activists to assume that Williams would carry through on her campaign promises. However, the activists remained engaged, which is a critical step to securing changes. You have to remain attentive to those who are put into office. It's not that they will renege on their promises but that they need to know that there is continued support for the issues that they ran on; otherwise, the daily duties of government will overshadow those issues.

As a result of activists remaining in touch with her, Williams became a strong ally for them, and within two years of being in office she got the council to create the Seattle Women's Commission in 1971 to address the issue of discrimination against women. She also received help from the newly elected mayor Wes Uhlman, who ran as a liberal Democrat committed to listening to groups, such as women, who had been ignored in the past.

Creating citizen commissions is an important step to integrating activists and their ideas into government. Although citizen commissions are only advisory, they can gain the ear of both politicians and the media. The Seattle Women's Commission originally consisted of fifteen volunteer members, with only a few women's-rights activists. As a result, feminist groups argued that commissioners should be chosen from a list that would be submitted by groups familiar with injustices toward women. That did not happen, but over time the commissioners whom the mayor and the council appointed were generally vetted by the groups advocating for women's rights.

The women's commission has served as a conduit, conveying programs, legislation, and projects to the attention of the council and the mayor. Those ideas often originate in women's groups operating outside the city government. The commission, housed in the Office for Civil Rights with dedicated staff, has become an inside advocate for outside concerns. They started with lobbying for an Equal Rights Amendment to the state constitution and for a bill that gave married women equal access to credit and community property. They succeeded in their first few years in requiring fair employment practices in city government with a city affirmative-action plan that explicitly protected women and gay people.

Since then the commission has lobbied councilmembers and held public educational forums about how women are impacted by practices both within and outside the city. In 2010, they helped pass city council legislation that created a policy of sweatshop-free labor standards for all bidders on city uniform contracts, since women are the primary workers being exploited in inhumane working conditions for abysmally low wages in other countries. They also were a critical player in convincing the city council to pass paid sick and safe time legislation in 2011, noting that the vast majority of the workers who would benefit were lower-wage women employees. And most recently they have focused on closing the gender wage gap, forming the Gender Equity in Pay Task Force, and allocating funding to implement task force recommendations.

While individual women activists could have also brought these issues to the council's attention, by forming a city commission citizen activists were able to consistently advocate for all women in a manner that carried more weight than what they could achieve as individuals. By becoming part of the system they did not sell out but gained power within government.

Out of the Closet

Opening the door for one group of citizens does not mean that others are being denied entry. In other words, gaining access to public power is not a zero-sum game; it is additive. That is why citizens supporting change in one field of interest should lend their support to citizens who also wish to change the status quo for their particular group. Protecting individuals' civil rights is an expansive notion.

For example, the advancement of gay rights directly benefited from women gaining more influence. The establishment of the Seattle Women's Commission contributed to establishing a commission for the gay community.

Twenty years after the Seattle Women's Commission was formed, the Seattle Commission for Sexual Minorities (SCSM) was founded in 1991. However, citizen activists had already pushed the City to take progressive steps to recognize gay rights in the early seventies. Lesbians led the way in 1973, when the Lesbian Resource Center's board requested that Councilmember Jeanette Williams and the Seattle Women's Commission support an ordinance to protect men and women from being fired or discriminated against just because they were gay or lesbian.

That year the council voted 8–1 to pass the new Fair Employment Practices Ordinance, specifying that sexual orientation was one of eleven categories where discrimination was prohibited. It was one of the first such ordinances in the nation, and even by 1980 only sixteen other cities and counties had passed legislation banning antigay discrimination in private and public workplaces.

As advocate groups become vocal, they catch the attention of politicians, particularly at election time, when citizen groups often endorse or rate candidates. Take advantage of those election debates and forums. There are often questions from the audience. Make sure you have advocates of your cause in the audience submitting questions to the candidates. If there is a demand for more direct citizen participation, press candidates for commitments to form a citizen's commission if there is none for that particular group.

Since the 1970s, there have been a number of groups that have advanced gay rights, but often their organizing tactics differ. One of the earliest organizations was the male-dominated Dorian Group, with a number of closeted gay members. They avoided publicity and preferred to influence decision makers by playing an inside game. They were initially businessmen, and under the leadership of Charlie Brydon, they hosted a gay-sponsored fundraiser for Mayor Wes Uhlman, who was seeking a new voting constituency to ward off a recall effort by the city's firefighters.

Their influence was challenged when the more activist Gay Liberation Front began in 1970. They preferred mobilizing the public, using megaphones at public demonstrations rather than quietly meeting in restaurants to influence politicians.

Each strategy had its advantages and both helped move gay rights into the public domain. While both faded away, other groups stepped forward, and in 1981 thirty-three men formed the Greater Seattle Business Association (GSBA) to produce a directory of their gay businesses.

The organization expanded beyond its Capitol Hill neighborhood, lesbians joined and became leaders, and GSBA became the voice for the gay business community. In refraining from confrontational tactics but continuing to present a public image, they combined the strategies used by the former groups. As a result the push for establishing a lesbian and gay citizens' commission picked up steam, and Mayor Charles Royer established the Gay and Lesbian Task Force in 1985, which eventually became the Seattle LGBT (Lesbian, Gay, Bisexual, and Transgender) Commission, a name that recognized the diversity that existed within the gay community. The term *LGBT community* has now largely replaced the term *gay community*. Over time the designation has been expanded to LGBTQ, to include the queer community, who are those who think of *queer* as an umbrella term that is more inclusive than assigning a more specific identity to an individual.

As a councilmember I saw how this assemblage of LGBTQ constituent groups, working through the citizen commission, was able to get the controversial Equal Benefits Ordinance passed in 1999. The *Seattle Times* editorial board had said the ordinance would cost the City money because it would require companies contracting with the City to extend the same benefits offered to married employees to employees with domestic partners. Citizens used the commission, working in alliance with Councilmember Tina Podlodowski, to follow up their success by strengthening the Fair Employment Practices Ordinance for all protected classes discriminated against in employment, including sexual minorities. Both successful efforts demonstrated that commissions could effectively reflect the interests of citizens who have grievances.

Political leaders who can listen to those concerns are also critical to success. They need to sponsor the needed legislation and convince other politicians that it is time to change the status quo. That calls for a coordinated strategy of having outside pressure groups work with inside politicians to get legislation passed. That approach worked not only for women and gay groups but also for the more recent immigrant rights movement.

Immigrant Rights

Intellectual discussions espousing theories feed and guide the development of political movements, but they do not create them. Actual living conditions give rise to grievances, which creates the opportunity to bring people together to solve them. Such were the conditions that gave birth to the immigrant rights movement of the twenty-first century when the percentage of our foreign-born population went from 4.7 percent in 1970 (which was a record low) to 12.9 percent in 2010 (the highest since 1930).

This wave of immigration is noticeable because we have not witnessed such a sustained increase for over a hundred years. It's not just that the percentage of immigrants has risen but that the percentage of immigrants who are recent arrivals is also high: over half of the foreign-born living in the United States today came here after 1990. They stand out as new residents and are often targets of suspicion by well-established populations. Fear of the unknown, like when a terrorist act occurs, can lead to stereotyping those who look or act differently from the majority of the population.

Immigrants easily identified as being from Muslim countries, as well as Sikh men, who always wear turbans, were being harassed as early as the 1990s. A number of Sikh taxi drivers were attacked by their passengers. Muslim schoolteachers began receiving threats. Even Muslim children were targeted by their schoolmates, and a third of Muslim families took their children out of public schools, according to a community leader. The situation became noticeably worse after the bombing of the World Trade Center on September 11, 2001.

Some citizens, fearful for those unjustly accused as a danger to our nation, became activists and demanded that recognizing human rights was at the core of our democracy. Pramila Jayapal was one such activist. Born and raised in India, Jayapal became a US citizen one years before 9/11. After that attack, she received calls from people in the community about more hate crimes occurring than ever before. In listening to the fear that others were living through, she felt that the United States, which was now her country, did not reflect the values that had made her want to be part of it.

Disturbed by these trends, she met with Seattle congressman Jim McDermott six days after 9/11. Jayapal had never met a politician before. She was very nervous about meeting him and felt that she had to hand him something to simply explain the problems that immigrants were facing. She quickly wrote out a short but broad mission statement saying that immigrants needed human services and advocacy but instead they were receiving hate. She typed across the top of a single sheet of paper, "Hate Free Zone of Washington."

A simple written statement like Jayapal's is a very important element to have when organizing. Have something short and to the point to hand the elected official who you are lobbying. Let them know what problem should be addressed. I have found that too many times constituents come to my office not sure what exact problem they want solved. They have concerns, fears, and gripes, but if they do not have a course of action to solve a particular problem, the elected official can easily express support but not follow up with actually doing something. Having something written down sharpens the discussion and leads directly to the next most important topic: what should be done.

And that was the question McDermott asked: "What should we do?" Jayapal had a clear, doable answer: hold a press conference—the next day. McDermott was taken aback by such a fast and bold move but quickly agreed to hold one. If you know what you want when you are lobbying, be prepared to ask for some action to be taken as soon as possible. Do not just ask for something that could be years off, because it will most likely get buried among all the other requests that are calling for more immediate attention.

Jayapal also asked other politicians to attend. Seattle city councilmember Judy Nicastro and I attended, along with King County councilmember Larry Gossett and others. We came to stand as one nation, undivided by religion or ethnicity. If you can get one politician to attend a public show of support for your issue, then invite others as well. Let them know that if they come, they will not be the only politician there. That makes a big difference for many, since standing as a lone politician on a controversial issue can be seen as too risky; some prefer to see which way the wind is blowing first. However, the more politicians that show up, the more likely it is that they will see that they in fact are fanning the winds of change.

At the press conference, Jayapal was not a featured speaker. She stood at the back of the crowd watching the event unfold. Congressman McDermott started handing out her one-page flyer and announced that a new organization had been formed to help immigrants. Jayapal later had to draw him aside and tell him that the organization was in fact "all in [her] head and only on that page." Another politician might have gotten angry and felt that he had been promoting a false promise, but McDermott calmly told her, "Well, you better start it now." And she immediately did.

By listening to the hopes of those in the immigrant community, she was able to present their concerns to higher authorities. She learned what other activists learn when they listen carefully: people are looking for someone to lead them and for a positive solution. Nobody liked what was happening to the immigrant community. They were looking for a way to take some positive action. A leader's passion and determination to do the right thing draws people in, especially in a troubled time. Jayapal, by working with others, provided a positive solution: create an organization called Hate Free Zone.

As more immigrants became involved, they found that by uniting with their friends, they could make a difference. They had to, because the government began targeting Muslim immigrants as suspected terrorists. The Patriot Act passed a month after 9/11. As Jayapal explained to the media, "Patriotism combined with fear is one of the most effective ways to suppress dissent and civil liberties."

Shortly after the act was signed into law, the US Customs Service raided the Somali-owned and -operated Maka Mini Mart in Seattle's Rainier Valley, the city's largest immigrant neighborhood and one of the poorest. The raid was part of President George W. Bush's crackdown on possible fronts for funding global terrorism, such as small grocery stores sending money overseas for Somali immigrants. In carrying out their raid, the FBI agents hauled off everything from business records to lettuce, fruit, and dinner rolls. The entire perishable inventory was loaded into trucks and sent to the dump. The allegations eventually proved groundless. But in the meantime, the Somali community was outraged that their ability to wire money to their relatives stuck in refugee camps had been stopped.

Hate Free Zone responded to the raid by holding rallies from the end of 2001 through the next year, supporting Somali grocery-store owners targeted by the federal government. It was not an easy step to take, for the Somali community had never been politically active or even held a rally. When many people become active, the social dynamics of a community change. In the Somali community new leadership roles emerged for women. At the rallies, the women initially stood at the back but gradually they came up to the microphone. They found that other women would stand up with them.

To draw the interest of the city government, they demonstrated that citizens outside of the Somali community were also concerned with how immigrants were being treated. By June of 2002 they had formed a broad coalition to urge the city council to prohibit all city employees from asking about immigration status.

To show that their coalition was more than just a list of names on a sheet of paper, they held a public hearing to air their experiences. Jayapal described how they had weekly organizing sessions, attended each time by twenty to thirty people from different ethnic communities representing some thirty organizations.

Just as Jayapal had learned by listening, she and others wanted government leaders to listen to them. In September 2002, Hate Free Zone, as part of a larger coalition, held the Justice for All hearing at Town Hall in Seattle. More than a thousand diverse community members attended. Sikhs, Somalis, Arabs, and Latinos, all people whose lives had changed since September 11, 2001, testified before a panel of invited elected officials. Hate Free Zone later renamed itself OneAmerica to reflect a powerful positive image of strength through diversity.

After the meeting at Town Hall, at the urging of the immigrant community, I introduced the "Don't Ask" legislation to the council in late fall of 2002. It codified what had been an informal city policy for dealing with the federal Immigration and Naturalization Service (INS). Although a few cities and states had similar policies, this legislation went further by actually making a law that clarified that while our police would cooperate with the federal government on criminal immigration violations, they would not enforce civil immigration violations; in effect, the law halted the drift toward federalizing our local police force.

In January 2003, Seattle City Council unanimously passed the "Don't Ask" legislation as one of the first ordinances in the nation prohibiting all city employees from asking about immigration status. While five other cities had policies that restricted police cooperation with the INS, only two others, New York City and San Francisco, actually had laws like the one Seattle adopted. It is much stronger to have an ordinance passed than to depend on a department's policies, because a department's policy could be changed when a new administration comes into office.

After the ordinance passed I got a call from the Hannity & Colmes nightly political talk show on Fox News Channel. I was invited to explain why my legislation didn't hinder President Bush's war on terrorism. On the show I appealed to Sean Hannity's sense of law and order by repeating what local police had often said: federalizing local police to enforce noncriminal federal immigration laws would reduce residents' willingness to talk to police for fear of being deported. The result is more crimes going unreported. Needless to say, I didn't convince Hannity, who went on to campaign against immigration reform for years afterward.

The push for immigrant rights continued in Seattle, as the council in 2005 directed the mayor to address services for the growing immigrant population. Receiving services is not the same as creating policy to direct government services. The next logical step was to establish a citizens' commission, similar to what had been formed for women and the LGBTQ community. The commission would allow for a continual and direct flow of communication to the city council and the mayor. The previous years of organizing paid off in 2007, when the City created an Immigrant and Refugee Advisory Council, recognizing that immigrants made up 16 percent of Seattle's population. The final step occurred in February 2012, when the council unanimously approved renaming the advisory group as the Seattle Immigrant and Refugee Commission. More importantly, it established the Office of Immigrant and Refugee Affairs as an executive department, with full-time paid staff dedicated to coordinating efforts across all city departments serving residents.

The pattern was the same in creating citizen commissions for women, gay people, and immigrants. Citizens recognized that their problems could be resolved only by government. They demanded that government adhere to its democratic principle of protecting the interests of all citizens—not in the limited legal sense, but in the classic one of universal equality of all people that this nation was founded upon. To achieve success, the laws must be changed, and that means having responsive and effective elected representatives working alongside citizen groups.

Jayapal said that the impetus for change must arise from the people; you cannot wait passively for someone else to do something. While each of these groups started outside the system, with the establishment of the citizen commissions, they have become part of the decision-making system. That alone does not guarantee continued success. Citizen commissions must continue to listen to their constituency; otherwise, they become part of the system tolerating injustices rather than fighting them.

CHAPTER 4

THE POWER IS IN THE DETAILS

The Columbia University Strike

A ctivists need more than slogans to change the practices of private and public institutions; they need to arm themselves with solid information to move others to join them. This was demonstrated to the nation when a student's library research precipitated the most explosive campus protest in the sixties. In March 1967, a Columbia University student who was a member of Students for a Democratic Society (SDS) came across documents in the international law library revealing the university's secret affiliation with the Institute for Defense Analyses (IDA), a think tank doing work for the US Department of Defense. The IDA worked with a consortium of twelve universities doing war research in evaluating the Pentagon's strategic weapons systems. Its executive committee had top-secret security clearance, and General Maxwell Taylor, head of the Joint Chiefs of Staff, was president of the IDA.

The relationship offered evidence of how universities could become part of the war machine by being embedded in the defense industry's military-planning process; they were no longer simply institutions of higher education. Uncovering official documents that the university's administration had previously denied solidified student suspicions into certified beliefs. The evidence was a powerful tool that forged student anger into a one-year campaign demanding that Columbia University's administration withdraw from the IDA. In March 1968 students peacefully demonstrated inside the Low Memorial Library administration building and gathered more than two thousand signatures for their petition. The administration responded by placing the six antiwar Columbia student activists who had led the petition effort on disciplinary probation.

That action galvanized more students to go on strike, and they took over five buildings by the end of April. The administration called in the police, who arrested over 700 students, with 148 of them sent to the hospital or in need of medical care. An outraged student body and faculty then joined the strike and closed down the university for the remainder of the year.

The TV networks provided visual images of the police beatings and the students occupying the university president's office, while newspapers' front pages portrayed SDS as the vanguard of the student revolution. However, the hard work of doing research and distributing it continued out of the limelight. Activists published a thirty-three-page in-depth analysis titled *Who Rules Columbia?*, which exposed in detail how military funding and corporate money played a major role in shaping Columbia's institutional mission. It inspired many students, like me, to realize that the power to change the status quo was just as likely to be found in libraries as in political rallies. Knowledge is power, and if used effectively, it can shape the future. In Columbia's case, knowledge led to the university severing its affiliation with the IDA.

Students Expose Sweatshop Providers

Forty-three years after students exposed Columbia University's corrupt practices, students are still challenging universities to act as institutions that are more responsible to the general public. Students at the University of Washington formed a local chapter of United Students Against Sweatshops, which focuses on stopping universities from contracting with companies that run sweatshops overseas to produce various articles of clothing bearing a university's logo. In 2010 the UW chapter started hearing from students at a number of campuses who were talking to workers about labor rights violations—serious health and safety problems, harassment, and intimidation—from Sodexo, one of the world's biggest concessionaires, which has a huge presence at campuses around the country. One of the chapter's leaders, Leo Baunach, explained that a feeling developed among their members that they needed to do something about it. That year they formed the Kick Out Sodexo Coalition.

Unlike the student-led research that kicked off the Columbia effort, in this case the students challenged university practices by citing information that would have been difficult for them as individuals to obtain. Sodexo's record of human, civil, and workers' rights violations in the United States were detailed in a report released by Human Rights Watch. This is a clear example of how national research organizations are critical to assisting citizen-led movements that seek institutional change. It is important as an activist to scan the Internet for organizations that are working in an area that you have an interest in affecting.

When beginning a major-issue campaign, it is also important to learn from similar efforts. Read reports and news releases to see what has worked elsewhere. As the UW students' anti-Sodexo campaign got underway, TransAfrica Forum, the nation's oldest African American policy organization promoting a just US foreign policy, published a report that greatly influenced the UW student effort. The students then modeled their efforts after the international solidarity campaigns that activists on campuses around the country had successfully run to stop the collegiate garment sector from dealing with companies that use sweatshops. Baunach said that, like these garment campaigns, they defined sweatshops broadly—as exploitation and abuse at work—so that Sodexo's practices domestically and internationally could both be addressed.

Even when using good information obtained from third-party sources, conducting local research is still necessary to see if that information applies to a particular situation or institution. UW students had to find out if the university had any contracts with Sodexo. When they found that Sodexo handled the university football team's (the Huskies) concessions, they began studying the inside workings of the university's decision-making process. Baunach explained, "On our own, we immersed ourselves in studying the contracting process at UW, from requests for proposals to contract renewal negotiations, and before the campaign got underway, we had a tight handle of the Sodexo contract with UW itself, both its legal content and the surrounding decision making."

The coalition's first step was to ask interim president Phyllis Wise to cut the university's relatively modest concessions contract with Sodexo. They targeted the university's president because the person in that position is the ultimate decision maker and can make change immediately. According to the coalition's leaders, the administration stalled them, treating their request to drop a comfortable business relationship as a minor nuisance.

The coalition then went to the student government and got them to pass a resolution supporting their request. It is an important step to try to get a public body, like the student government or the city council, to issue a statement of support for your efforts. If you fail to win the support of the entire organization, try to get at least some of its members to sign a statement. Over the course of the UW students' two-year anti-Sodexo campaign, more than twenty organizations on and off campus, ranging from church groups to student groups to politicians, like me, sent signed letters of support to the university.

During this time, students put additional pressure on the administration by holding several sit-ins, beginning with the president's office, which led to twenty-seven students being arrested. Undeterred, they held two more sit-ins, one in the athletic director's office and another in the admissions office, with additional students being arrested.

Finally, in the spring of 2011 the university created a committee to investigate the allegations and concluded that Sodexo wasn't an evil company, but it had a few problems that it was working on. However, thanks to extensive research, students and citizens became aware of the inhumane working conditions that they were indirectly sustaining by allowing Sodexo to do business with a public university. In response to that growing concern, the university finally switched concessionaires when Sodexo's contract expired that December.

During this same period, my office worked closely with the Washington Fair Trade Coalition, which had been assisting the UW students, to adopt similar sweatshop-free labor standards for all bidders on city uniform contracts. In 2010, the City integrated these standards into contracts and new bids. Sharing information between university and city activists around a common issue bolstered each of our efforts by demonstrating that contracting with companies that relied on sweatshop practices affected both universities and cities.

Ticketing Aggressive Panhandling

Panhandling, a common sight in Seattle's central business district, had many downtown residents, businesses, and visitors wanting to see it banned. More complaints were received by the city council over time as new condominiums went up downtown, bringing in thousands of new residents, many of whom had lived in the suburbs or in quiet residential neighborhoods with few people on the streets begging for money.

In response the city council, by a 5–4 vote in April 2010, passed legislation providing a broad definition of aggressive panhandling and allowing it to be ticketed.

The law's sponsor, public safety chair Tim Burgess, said, "It's about our city saying together we will no longer tolerate this aggressive and intimidating behavior." However, aggressive panhandling was already a crime. The new law expanded the definition of panhandling and ticketed a wider range of activity. Many of those who objected to panhandling wanted to ban it altogether, but the city attorney cautioned that a ban would probably not hold up in the courts because it would violate constitutional rights.

The main task of the citizens opposing the new law was to expose as false the underlying assumption that aggressive panhandling was rampant. When attempting to convince councilmembers or, for that matter, any elected representative not to support a bad piece of legislation, attack the assumption that this legislation is necessary.

In this instance, the role of research was significant in challenging the legislation's implication that most panhandling involved aggressive solicitation. A 2009 survey of residents in the greater downtown area was initially cited in support of the legislation. When a poll or a survey is cited as evidence, get a copy of the entire findings and the questions asked. Often I've found that the results are cherry-picked to support a particular position. By obtaining the original material, you can open the debate up by showing that other data collected from the same source could point to a different conclusion. And this is what happened when activists reviewed the survey used to back up the legislation.

The survey revealed that while 66 percent of the respondents were concerned about aggressive solicitation, a nearly equal percentage (63 percent) of respondents were concerned about all panhandling. The survey also showed, contrary to the rationale used to justify the legislation, that "almost all residents continue to feel safe walking downtown during the day" and "perceptions of nighttime safety are stable." Finally, the central business district saw an improvement in the area of aggressive panhandling, with 57 percent of those polled concerned in 2007 and only 32 percent concerned in 2009. People may not like panhandling, but nonaggressive panhandling is a protected civil right.

Activists next scoured through the police records and discovered that the combined rates of assault and robbery—the sort of person-on-person crime that would be associated with street disorder—dropped slightly downtown between 2008 and 2009. Ironically, Pioneer Square, the neighborhood with the most panhandlers and social services, saw the smallest increase in crime in the past year, while the rates of assaults and robberies actually dropped. Meanwhile, nearly 80 percent of those charged under the existing law against aggressive panhandling in the previous ten years had received a conviction of some kind. A memo from Seattle police chief John Diaz to Councilmember Burgess came to light saying that there were enough laws already on the books.

In reviewing the information gathered by activists and organizations that represented the poorest citizens, the Seattle Human Rights Commission, a citizen board appointed by the city council and mayor to make recommendations on public policy, voted unanimously to oppose the council's legislation. They said that the data was "insufficient to support the substance of the proposed ordinance." Ticketing panhandlers was shown to be more about suppressing panhandlers than lowering criminal activity.

The cumulative impact of this information helped Mayor McGinn veto the council's legislation—a rare occurrence, there having been only seven mayoral vetoes in the previous twenty years. Without the data to support the assumptions underlying the need for ticketing panhandling, Burgess was unable to secure the six votes needed to override the mayor's veto, and the legislation was defeated.

Passing Paid Sick Leave

When activists asked me in the spring of 2011 to sponsor legislation mandating businesses to provide paid sick leave, my reaction was one of both sympathy and healthy skepticism. That's a great goal, I said, knowing that 135 other countries already had mandated paid sick days for their entire workforce. Nevertheless, I cautioned that it was not likely that we'd see it anytime soon. In less than nine months I was shown to be wrong. Not only was there popular support for the issue and well-organized advocate groups pushing it, there was also a wealth of data to prove to public officials that the sky would not fall if paid sick leave legislation was passed and that in fact we would all be better off with it.

Advocates for the legislation went to the nonprofit Economic Opportunity Institute (EOI) for assistance. The institute's policy director, Marilyn Watkins, compiled data from existing government sources, which showed that there were roughly 190,000 people working in Seattle without paid sick leave. The campaign then had to make the case that the public should be concerned. It's not enough to argue that the humanitarian needs of a particular set of workers are not being met. For the cause to take root in the public consciousness, it's important to show why the disinterested should be concerned. The line of reasoning presented was that sick workers handling your food, your groceries, or your personal items in your home while caring for your loved ones would spread diseases, from the common cold to much more serious illnesses.

The EOI, working with unions like SEIU and UFCW (United Food and Commercial Workers International Union), took the next step by showing data that showed this threat was real. They found that one in four grocery workers reports coming to work sick when they don't have paid sick leave. With 78 percent of accommodation and food-service workers, about half of retail workers, and one-fourth of health-care workers not earning paid sick days, chances are they are going to work sick. In King County, from 2006 to 2010 about 30 percent of recent foodborne-illness outbreaks (almost all due to norovirus) were linked to food handlers who worked while sick. The message delivered to the city council was simple: sick people make healthy people sick; you don't want to be around them.

Some opponents said workers would use their entire paid sick leave time to take extended vacations. That accusation was quickly countered by citing a study commissioned by the City of San Francisco that evaluated their paid sick leave after it had been enforced since February 2007.

It is important when working with elected representatives to include an evaluation component to any new program proposed. This accomplishes two things. First, it helps get the votes needed to pass the legislation. Those councilmembers who are supportive but concerned about possible negative impacts can find comfort in knowing that a study of the new legislation's impact will be conducted. Second, the data collected is useful for activists in other cities, as it helps them show how the business climate in another city adapted to the proposed legislation.

This is exactly what happened in Seattle. The council and media saw how the typical worker in San Francisco used only three days of paid sick leave a year even though they have on average nine days available to them. Surprisingly, 25 percent of the employees with access to paid sick leave didn't use it. The San Francisco report was the most valuable tool in addressing the concerns of both employers and employees about how Seattle's businesses might be impacted by required paid sick leave. The independent evaluation of San Francisco's paid sick leave law revealed that since the law was enacted, San Francisco has had a stronger job market than the surrounding counties and the state as a whole, including in the restaurant industry, which was most impacted by the ordinance.

The paid sick leave campaign was effective not only because good data existed but also because organizations dedicated staff to digging the data up and then quickly responding to critics. The EOI's Marilyn Watkins provided much of the research needed. The local unions SEIU 775, UFCW 21, and Teamsters Local 117 all dedicated staff to delivering the information to their members, the public, and most importantly to the city councilmembers. Without their paid staff responding to hostile editorials and personally meeting with policy makers, the debate would have veered into scaremongering rather than looking at the facts.

The council voted 8–1 to pass the most extensive paid sick leave law in the nation, due in part to the level of confidence they had in the research showing that businesses would continue to prosper and workers would be healthier and more efficient in carrying out their jobs.

Tracking Hate Crimes

Even without initiating legislation, the collection and presentation of data in itself can be a powerful organizing tool in shaping public policy. An individual presenting his or her own research can alter the political landscape. Such was the case in 2006, when Ken Molsberry presented a bias crimes and incident report summarizing Seattle Police Department data from 2000 to 2005 to the Public Safety, Civil Rights, and Technology Committee, which I chaired.

Molsberry was working as a data analyst for the Seattle City Attorney's Office when, a week before Christmas 2004, he read a story in the *Seattle Gay News* headlined, "Perceived to Be Gay . . . and Bashed for It." The incident occurred in

Molsberry's neighborhood, Ballard, and being gay, he wanted to find out how often bias crimes were committed throughout the city. These are criminal acts committed against a person because of that person's real or perceived characteristics (race, religion, sexual orientation, etc.). Bias crimes, often referred to as hate crimes in the media, victimize every member of the targeted group.

Being comfortable with collecting and analyzing data, Molsberry began his own research. He had difficulty in accessing information from the police department, so in his personal time he started filing public records requests. After eighteen months, his report was complete, and he called my office to see if I was interested in seeing it. I said of course and invited him to present his findings to my committee so that the public would know what was happening in their city. As he wrote in his report, "Knowing about a problem is the first step in solving it. And while local law enforcement is well aware of the problem—and the pattern—of bias attacks in Seattle, citizens generally are not."

Molsberry identified 403 bias-motivated attacks throughout the city, ranging from verbal threats to physical threats to actual physical harm. In all instances, the victims were targeted because of protected classifications such as race, religion, sexual orientation, and national origin. More than a quarter of them were antigay incidents, and they occurred throughout the city. Upon reviewing the report, the police department verified the accuracy of the raw data he had obtained.

I followed up on Molsberry's report by joining two other councilmembers in requesting that our city auditor review police records on bias crimes. Subsequently, the auditor recommended that police officers attend regular refresher training on bias crimes and incidents and record bias crimes and incidents in their reports, and that the police department collect that data and make it public. The auditor's follow-up report in 2010 found that the police had implemented those changes. If a citizen had not collected the original data and made it public, police practices most likely would have continued to inadequately measure the number of bias crimes and incidents, endangering the lives of those in the LGBTQ community as well as ethnic minorities and women.

Networking Information

The most powerful means to collect and disseminate information is through a network linking many data sources. Certainly, libraries serve that purpose as well as Google searches. While those are information-rich reservoirs, they are not interactive, with multiple users. If you are researching an issue or organizing an effort, one of the first things you should do is see if other organizations have been active in the same area. Go to their websites and see if they are members of any national associations. Also, check local websites and print publications that may list groups that have a relevant connection to your issue.

For an information network to be effective, it must provide knowledge that is timely, accurate, and relevant. It must also allow organizers to exchange and update that information as needed. The advent of Internet search engines has replaced the era when activists used directories and even community newspapers to distribute information for organizing purposes. For instance, in 1973, I pulled together a dozen students to publish five thousand copies of the *People's Yellow Pages*, a hundred-page guide to social services, community groups, and activist organizations, for a retail price of seventy-five cents. We used the proceeds to start a community newspaper, the *Seattle Sun*. I soon realized that these attempts did not create a dynamic network for gathering and exchanging information. First, by the time the *People's Yellow Pages* hit the streets, some of the information was out of date. Second, even an up-to-date weekly newspaper, while providing current information to the public, was not designed to share information among organizations.

In the political realm, the two major political parties try to keep their members informed, and in turn their members try to influence the party's agenda. In the world of citizen activist movements, there is no one depository or network, since there are so many issues and organizations. Nevertheless, within each issue area there are often national organizations and associations that can provide both information and assistance to local start-up efforts.

When individual students at the University of Washington wanted to challenge the university's reliance on corporations engaged in sweatshop practices, they did not have to do original research. The national organization United Students Against Sweatshops was there to provide not only data but also examples of how other successful campus campaigns had been conducted.

When residents in the Georgetown neighborhood wanted to stop a flow of trucks and trains carrying waste through their community, they found allies in national groups like the Sierra Club and Environment America. Those organizations had dedicated staff doing research to promote zero waste, which full-time working families did not have the time to do.

When grocery workers and home health-care workers wanted the right to stay home sick without losing pay, the Economic Opportunity Institute and the Center for American Progress provided hard data to demonstrate that businesses could survive and prosper with paid sick leave laws.

In these citizen-led efforts, the underlying principle that allowed each to be successful was the recognition that the citizens were not alone. There is a large and diffuse array of national and regional organizations willing to help citizens; they just need to be contacted.

After becoming a councilmember, I had expected to discover such a network of organizations that could help public officials collect data to shape public policy. I attended the annual meeting of the National League of Cities (NLC), the largest organization in the country connecting municipal governments. I thought it would have an information network to find and compare relevant laws in various cities. While there were a half-dozen different interest groups influencing NLC's congressional lobbying agenda, there was no single network for elected officials to share information on policies and practices. For instance, I wanted to find out how many cities had established citizen commissions dealing specifically with women's, immigrants', and LGBTQ issues. There was no list or way to compile such a list from searching a database.

However, two national networks for information sharing came to my attention, both primarily focused on helping state legislators, not city officials or citizens. The American Legislative Exchange Council (ALEC) was co-founded in 1973 by Henry Hyde, who went on to become a congressman and to sponsor the Hyde Amendment, which limited women's rights to abortion. The other founder was conservative activist Paul Weyrich, who coined the term *moral majority*. Over forty years later, ALEC has more than thirty-five full-time employees devoted to limiting government and promoting free markets.

Unlike ALEC's conservative agenda, the American Legislative and Issue Campaign Exchange (ALICE), established in 2012, had sustainability and equality as its core values, says its founder, Joel Rogers. It did not accept corporate contributions, had a much smaller staff, and was more of a depository for information than an advocate for political change, as is ALEC. Rogers merged ALICE with the

Progressive States Network (PSN) and founded the State Innovation Exchange (SiX) to more closely follow ALEC's model of directly facilitating the introduction and passage of new legislation. SiX proudly states on its website, "We're building the legislative wing of the progressive movement."

President Obama has said that cities are at the forefront of pursuing innovative and progressive legislation. Since he has taken office, cities have adopted laws and programs that the federal government and the state legislatures have avoided—for example, paid sick leave, higher minimum wage, recycling laws, and affordable housing. Because cities usually operate in isolation from each other, activists as well as councilmembers and mayors could use a network to facilitate cooperation among cities. Having gotten a dozen other city councils to pass resolutions asking President Obama to create an advisory group to his newly created Office of Urban Affairs, which resided in his Executive Offices in 2011, I had a list of councilmembers from various cities who shared my vision. Despite my visit to the White House to discuss this proposal, it came to naught.

Frustrated, I contacted councilmembers as well as organizations that pushed progressive municipal policies and invited them to a meeting to explore forming a national progressive municipal network. On March 9, 2012, over thirty people, representing eight cities and fourteen organizations, met at the Center for American Progress to discuss the proposal. The participants agreed to pursue creating such a network, and in the fall of 2012, Local Progress, a national municipal policy network, was created. By the time of the third annual meeting in 2014, there were about four hundred self-identified progressive elected municipal officials working with community-based organizations to further social and economic justice issues such as minimum-wage legislation. And the network continues to grow, assisting both public officials and community groups in exchanging information that enables them to better tackle common problems.

National networks are critical to providing politicians and activists with the most current information on what policies and projects are being tried and are working in other cities. They must also be open to the public so that knowledge is not concentrated in the hands of politicians and anyone who has access will be able to use the network's information to transform his or her own community.

CHAPTER 5
CHANGE IS A MARATHON

Getting to Same-Sex Marriage

When the Washington State Legislature passed Senator Ed Murray's bill legalizing same-sex marriages at the beginning of 2012, it seemed almost unbelievable. Forty-three years earlier two males in their twenties applied for a marriage certificate in Seattle. They were refused, of course. They then fought for the right to be married through the state courts but lost in the end. The path toward same-sex marriages was a long one, and it led to success only because there were citizens who kept trudging away on it for years.

Over time the gay movement came to be referred to more often as the LGBTQ movement to recognize the diversity of the community. Paralleling this change, activists also began to reach out to those outside the LGBTQ community. Activists encouraged gay people to present opportunities to have discussions with those in the straight world about common concerns, such as having safe, secure families. For example, placing a family photograph on your desk could prompt that conversation.

To the media, more than anyone else, same-sex marriage became the holy grail for recognizing the rights of those in the LGBTQ community. But the reality was far more complex. Activists in that community tell a story of many battles but also one of steady progress spanning over four decades. The strategies they employed varied from quietly negotiating details with politicians in small restaurants to literally shouting outside those establishments, demanding attention for the AIDS epidemic. It took a combination of tactics, personalities, and groups to eventually secure health benefits, job security, open housing, public safety, and yes, in the end, same-sex marriage.

Through this long struggle for same-sex marriage, ultimately ending in success in Washington State, there are a few lessons that can be learned, with one note of caution. Since state constitutions vary, strategies must be shaped to each state's legal framework. For instance, Washington's constitution cannot be amended by a popular vote, unlike thirty other states where that is possible and where they have been amended to ban same-sex marriages. It was a Karl Rove strategy under George W. Bush to turn out conservative voters. However, Washington did have a statewide vote to overturn the state legislation legalizing same-sex marriages.

When I talked to citizens in the LGBTQ community and asked what central condition had to be maintained in order to achieve success, the answer often came down to being dedicated to the long game, keeping people involved year after year no matter what particular setbacks were dealt to them. This is applicable to any movement seeking to change the status quo. In the case of fighting for LGBTQ civil rights, adhering to some key principles made this endurance possible.

Mentioned often was an understanding among the movement leaders that their struggle was about the community's welfare, not any individual's ego. It is not about being on TV or in the paper; it's about getting the message across. As one leader also told me, it's not about winning the debate, but moving the public to accept your point as legitimate. As an example, in order to reach the broadest audience, movement leaders chose a speaker from the League of Women Voters rather than an LGBTQ speaker to appear on a TV show to defend same-sex marriages.

It is also important to have multiple fronts. Anne Levinson, one of the early LGBTQ leaders, said, "Having strong advocate groups who set the outer limits makes other changes more acceptable. Pushing the envelope is necessary and critical, but it carries risks." One prime example of a group taking the direct-action approach was ACT UP (AIDS Coalition to Unleash Power), the most well-known national group to demand public assistance and corporate cooperation in combating AIDS.

Seattle's ACT UP chapter was founded in 1988. One of their first acts was to demonstrate against Safeway stores because they refused to sell an issue of a pop music magazine, *Spin*, because it included a condom along with an article about safe sex, an issue that obviously affected more than just those in the LGBTQ community. The chapter members were willing to take power into their own hands. When local government agencies could not move fast enough to stop the transmission of AIDS through needle use, they started a needle exchange for intravenous drug users in 1989. This was several months before the health department finally received permission to do so. Just the threat of an ACT UP demonstration outside an opening night party at the Seattle Art Museum was enough to make one of the museum's board members withdraw his zoning complaint to halt the construction of an AIDS rest home in the residential Madison Valley neighborhood.

Lifelong activist and co-founder of ACT UP Seattle Phil Bereano said their activist strategy was critical for "challenging and publicly taunting the powers that be" in order to change history. He believes that ACT UP allowed people to do something positive with their grief over personal losses and their anger with the social injustices that flowed from AIDS.

Despite the different tactics pursued by the various fronts of the LGBTQ community, all of them were united in changing the laws to extend to them the civil rights enjoyed by all citizens in our democracy. Washington State's legalizing same-sex marriage was preceded by significant other changes in Seattle's municipal law. In 1989 Seattle was the first city in the nation to extend sick and funeral leave benefits to the domestic partners of city employees. The experience gained by activists in that and other efforts helped them craft a winning strategy for statewide efforts.

Levinson explained, "We got to marriage in this state because there had been so many prior battles requiring us to build coalitions that the process created a broad base. We had changed the landscape in Washington." They built coalitions by not writing off some people who they would ordinarily have put into boxes labeled "Opponents." Instead, they sought common links with them and assumed the best in their critics. As members of a discriminated minority group, the LGBTQ leaders felt that they needed every ally to get legislation passed.

That tactic came to the fore in 2006, when it stopped two statewide initiative efforts. The initiatives would have reversed an antidiscrimination law protecting gay men and lesbians that had passed the Washington State Legislature that year. The LGBTQ activists found that seniors were natural allies in fighting these measures, because some seniors could have lost their social security benefits from a prior marriage. Through a broad coalition, activists ran a statewide "decline to sign" campaign, which encouraged voters not to sign the initiatives, thus denying them the opportunity to be placed on the ballot.

The campaign was a success, and both initiatives were kept off the ballot.

The following year, Ed Murray became a state senator. Since he lacked the votes to change the marriage laws, he successfully worked the legislature to pass a domestic partnership law. In 2009, he worked with other legislators to pass legislation that further extended the rights and responsibilities of domestic partners. These efforts were a deliberate strategy to gain as much ground as possible in preparation for passing legislation for same-sex marriage.

As Murray and his supporters persistently took incremental steps, additional allies were brought on board, particularly as they could see how the LGBTQ community members were being treated. Churches, synagogues, businesses, community groups, and schools all became part of a growing coalition that had been formed through previous campaigns. Corporations like Microsoft and Boeing financially supported the 2012 pro–Referendum 74 campaign, which confirmed the state legislation legalizing same-sex marriages. A new Catholic organization was created that year, Catholics for Marriage Equality Washington State, to raise a public Catholic voice in support of the referendum. Meanwhile, the Roman Catholic Church opposed same-sex marriages.

The final victory came when a phenomenal turnout of 80 percent of Washington State voters went to the polls to approve the referendum.

On November 6, 2012, Washington, Maine, and Maryland became the first states to legalize same-sex marriage through popular vote.

Activists had followed the golden rule: treat others how you'd want to be treated. In asking others to keep an open mind, they kept theirs open as well. As a result, over the course of four decades, they moved public opinion to acknowledge that every citizen deserves to have the same rights.

Legalizing Marijuana

In November 2012, Washington State and Colorado became the only two states to legalize personal use of marijuana for adults twenty-one and over. Like the vote to allow same-sex marriages, legalizing marijuana took more than four decades of incremental steps to achieve. In both instances, the voters were clearly on their side; same-sex marriage received 54 percent of the vote, and legalizing marijuana got 56 percent.

Many people have been arrested for smoking marijuana or know someone who has been. As recently as 2010, marijuana arrests accounted for 52 percent of all drug arrests, with nearly eight million people arrested on pot charges since 2000. And 88 percent of those arrests were for simple possession.

With so many arrests, there soon developed an overlapping interest in legalizing marijuana among libertarians and liberals as well as advocates of privacy rights and civil rights. The principle of emphasizing common goals, as was practiced by those advocating for same-sex marriages, made the success of legalizing marijuana possible. Building alliances leads to victory.

Enforcing marijuana laws has been used as a political means for stifling leftist dissent. This was most evident in the late sixties as the federal government, working with local jurisdictions, arrested local antiwar and civil rights leaders for just possessing marijuana. One of the more outrageous examples of this practice was when the poet and political activist John Sinclair, a founding member of the White Panther Party, an antiracist socialist group, received ten years in federal prison for possessing two joints in 1968. The prior year two student friends who were active in SDS were arrested when a single joint was found in their home. They pleaded guilty and spent a year in jail.

However, on the right, libertarian conservatives William F. Buckley and Milton Friedman supported legalizing marijuana. Buckley made a strong case for legalizing medical marijuana, since taking medication is at the heart of the private relationship between patients and doctors. He noted in 2004 that every state ballot initiative to legalize medical marijuana had been approved.

Data also began to mount on how enforcing marijuana laws was resulting in a disproportionately high number of young black people ages eighteen to twenty-five being arrested, even though white youth in that same age bracket were using marijuana more frequently. According to the Department of Justice, data collected nationwide between 1980 and 2010 showed that police arrested black youth for drug crimes at more than twice the rate that they arrested white youth.

In response to these trends, the national groups NORML and the Marijuana Policy Project were formed. They argued that the national war on drugs fostered an unjust legal system that was a waste of taxpayers' dollars, while marijuana posed far fewer health risks than alcohol or tobacco. Those arguments had made headway in the seventies. On a national level, President Jimmy Carter had called for decriminalizing the possession of marijuana.

In Seattle, from the start of Mayor Charles Royer's three terms in 1978, he publicly said that too many people were going to jail for a minor offense and that marijuana possession should be the lowest priority for arrests. He had been elected on a platform of promoting human rights and felt that it was a moral issue. The independently elected city attorney, Republican Doug Jewett, supported Royer. However, the police chief opposed the idea of the mayor and the council determining how the police should enforce laws, and enforcement continued as it had in the past.

Seattle citizen activists were not organized enough to alter this dynamic. Royer admitted that even in the black community, which was beginning to withstand the worst of drug enforcement, legalizing marijuana did not have a high priority among the many issues they were concerned with. Even having politicians promote an issue is not good enough. They need community backing to sustain their efforts in fighting off arguments from other politicians opposing change. Electing someone to office is only opening the door for change; politicians need citizens to organize to push legislation through it.

Sometimes issues rise to the top of the public's consciousness because they dovetail with other ones that they have no immediate relationship to. This happened when the rise of AIDS resulted in the demand to provide medical marijuana to lessen the pain for those suffering from the syndrome. The gay community was most effective in making that demand. Although AIDS was identified with the gay community, early in the 1980s health authorities realized that nearly half of the people with AIDS were not homosexual men. However, gay people had a cohesive community that had just begun to exercise some political muscle. Just as AIDS made its appearance in Seattle, the gay business network formed the Greater Seattle Business Association, and Mayor Royer created the Gay and Lesbian Task Force.

While the gay community advocated for using marijuana for medical uses, cancer patients began to see how marijuana could relieve their pain as well. Both of these communities benefited from Jack Herer's 1985 nonfiction book *The Emperor Wears No Clothes*, which armed marijuana advocates with facts to attack its prohibition on scientific grounds. As with global warming, scientific arguments began to replace myths and unverifiable assumptions. Reliable data supplied activists with the facts they needed to sweep away the fears opponents of legalizing medical marijuana fanned.

Herer appeared as one of the earliest speakers at Hempfest, an annual gathering of marijuana advocates spurred on through the efforts of its founder, Vivian McPeak. Their first gathering at Capitol Hill's Volunteer Park in 1991 attracted five hundred people; the following year two thousand came. Hempfest has continued to grow almost exponentially. By 2013 it had become a three-day annual political rally, concert, and arts and crafts fair with attendance typically over 450,000 at Myrtle Edwards Park alongside Puget Sound. Speakers over the years have included actor and activist Woody Harrelson and former chief of the Seattle Police Department Norm Stamper. In 2002, I spoke there and received a Green Ribbon Award for excellence in cannabis activism. I also played a role in helping Hempfest retain its park site despite city staff arguing for moving it to a less convenient location.

Hempfest served as a great opportunity to inform the participants of efforts to legalize marijuana and to solicit volunteers in that effort. Throwing parties and celebrations is critical not only for maintaining momentum but also for giving people a sense that they are part of something larger than themselves. That community became a powerful political force in challenging the Washington Supreme Court's 1997 *Seeley v. State* decision to deny a terminal cancer patient the right to use medical marijuana. The greater Hempfest community mobilized citizens across the state, both in conservative- and liberal-leaning counties, and a tidal wave of support reversed that decision, passing State Initiative 692 with

59 percent of the vote. After November 1998, the use of medical marijuana became legal in Washington.

That same month Alaska, Nevada, Oregon, and Arizona also voted to legalize marijuana for medical use. According to *Governing Magazine*, as of April 2015, twenty-three states and the District of Columbia currently have laws legalizing marijuana in some form, with four of them legalizing marijuana for recreational use. Still, the federal government has not recognized marijuana use as a legal activity despite an ABC News poll in January 2010 showing that 81 percent of Americans believe that medical cannabis should be legal.

The next step that activists wanted to pursue was legalizing marijuana for recreational adult use. Bruce Ramsey was a columnist and on the editorial staff of the *Seattle Times*. He describes himself as a kind of libertarian who smoked in college. Medical concerns played a major role in his supporting legalization of marijuana, but a number of his fellow conservatives opposed legalizing medical marijuana for fear that it would open the door to full legalization. He laughed and told me, "I guess they were right."

In 2000, two years after medical marijuana was legalized, Fred Noland, the president of the King County Bar Association (KCBA), the largest county bar association in the state, wrote an editorial lamenting the failure of the war on drugs. Editorials from prominent legal professionals can motivate their colleagues to action. If you can get one to write an editorial, circulate it to mobilize those who have the resources to highlight your issue. In this instance, Noland's piece prompted the KCBA to initiate a legal task force to explore drug law reforms. Having well-researched reports from the legal community can grab the attention of politicians and journalists, which is what happened with the bar association's release of a major report in 2001, *Is It Time to End the War on Drugs?* The report concluded that current drug policy was flawed and generating numerous negative societal consequences.

Dominic Holden, a freelance journalist at the alternative weekly the *Stranger*, followed up this work in 2003 by forming the Sensible Seattle Coalition and instigating Initiative 75, which required the Seattle Police Department and the city attorney's office to make arrest and prosecution of marijuana offenses the lowest law enforcement priority.

Victories breed optimism, so it is generally preferable to go for a more likely victory than chancing a more likely defeat. Holden could have designed an initiative to decriminalize marijuana altogether, but that would have invited a larger risk of losing. Instead, by just making possession of marijuana the lowest priority for enforcement, he was able to minimize opposition and the initiative passed.

This victory further motivated the legal community to ask the state legislature to establish a special consultative body composed of public officials, civic leaders, and experts to recommend a regulatory system for the control of psychoactive substances. It was a seemingly small step, but it kept the issue before the state legislators and offered a discussion topic for citizen lobbyists.

Businessperson Greta Carter became one of the citizen lobbyists. She had met with me for advice and I suggested that it would help to show politicians that the emerging cannabis industry could regulate itself. She soon founded CCSE, the Coalition for Cannabis Standards and Ethics, to guide medical marijuana growers and distributors by adopting common standards of operations. Her first meeting to create CCSE had forty people, the next one had sixty people, and soon she had over a hundred. From the faces of the participants she saw that people began to feel empowered by meeting together and planning how to enter the political arena. After several meetings, they set off to the state legislature to let them know that they were responsible tax-paying businesses.

In 2011, state senator Jeanne Kohl-Wells, working with CCSE, the American Civil Liberties Union (ACLU), and other groups, was able to get the state legislature to pass legislation creating a sensible production and distribution system for legalized medical marijuana. Unfortunately, Governor Christine Gregoire's partial vetoes made the legislation practically inoperable. Ironically, her veto motivated the advocate community to come together and push for outright legalization of marijuana, since the state government had failed to come up with a workable arrangement.

After years of activists' dispersing information on the positive effects of marijuana and on the evidence that many youths, particularly black youths, were needlessly going to jail, public sentiment dramatically shifted away from a prohibition mentality. This shift was most evident when the publisher of the state's largest newspaper, the *Seattle Times*, known for having a rock-solid probusiness stance, ran an editorial endorsing its legalization.

The range of public acceptance was evident when the former US attorney John McKay and the current Seattle city attorney Pete Holmes helped sponsor the Initiative 502 campaign to legalize recreational marijuana. Their involvement lent the campaign establishment credibility. The ACLU brought along the civil rights community by loaning one of their top staff, Alison Holcomb, to run the campaign organization.

The most vocal opposition came from a section of the prolegalization community saying that the initiative would hinder true legalization. In particular, they vehemently opposed making it a crime to drive if an amount of marijuana above a particular level was detected in the bloodstream, since it could discourage medical patients from seeking marijuana treatments. As a result, the marijuana community was divided, and major players like Hempfest and CCSE stayed neutral.

Even before this division occurred, Douglas Hiatt, a longtime marijuana defense attorney, sued the City in 2011 over legislation that I had sponsored requiring that medical marijuana dispensaries and grow operations comply with all local permit regulations applicable to similar activities. Hiatt charged that these laws could potentially incriminate those in the medical marijuana business. However, the majority of marijuana businesses welcomed the legislation, since it offered greater certainty in complying with the City's various regulations. The court threw out Hiatt's case in 2012. After Initiative 502 passed, I co-sponsored legislation designating which zones marijuana businesses could be located in. That legislation was not challenged in the courts.

The above legislative process dealing with permits and zoning laws may seem to be far removed from the concerns of activists. But this level of detail determines how successful a group is in achieving its objectives. When legislation is being written, it is important to pay attention. Ask for draft copies of the legislation or at least summaries of it from politicians or city staff so that you know what is being considered. Knowledge is power; obtain it and you gain power to help shape the legislation you are seeking.

Activists succeeded in legalizing marijuana because they crafted a rational message that appealed to a variety of groups. Emphasizing taxpayers' savings and the unjust enforcement of the laws attracted both fiscal conservatives and human rights advocates. Mixing in a pinch of libertarians, who advocated that the state should keep its nose out of their homes, and aging baby boomers, who recalled smoking weed in their college days, added to the breadth of support. When they all recognized that they shared a common interest, a powerful political realignment cut across traditional party lines, dramatically altering our laws and culture.

CHAPTER 6
GET THE WORD OUT

While speeches can arouse passion and move groups to act, to involve more people and to sustain their involvement, you have to get the word out. There are many types of media activists can use to convey a message, and each has its unique advantages. Know them in order to be effective.

I'll cover a wide range of media to spread a message, starting with printed-word formats, not social media. Though social media has gained popularity throughout the world because it distributes information far more quickly and widely than either print or traditional over-the-waves media (TV and radio), print media is still a substantial medium for reaching people. And often it is more effective than social media in organizing. It cannot be ignored.

Books

Books, whether in print or electronic format, involve a significant investment to produce and require readers to commit a substantial amount of time. Students, who have the obligation to study and read, are an ideal market for books, whose influence on them can shape their perceptions of society and their desire to change it. I experienced this firsthand as an active participant in the student movement of the sixties. Three massively popular books reframed the uncritical acceptance of the fifties and helped feed the desire to create a better democracy: C. Wright Mills's *The Power Elite*, Senator John F. Kennedy's bestseller *Profiles in Courage*, and Michael Harrington's *The Other America*.

The Power Elite postulated that those who managed the political, military, and economic institutions shared a common agenda. Although it avoided a conspiracy approach, it did highlight the existence of coordinated elites protecting the status quo. President Eisenhower in his last national address even warned the nation of such a powerful "military-industrial complex." *Profiles in Courage* made heroes of those who pursued justice in the face of mass criticism. In glorifying those who stood up for their beliefs, it justified the pursuit of seeking the right solutions without compromise. *The Other America* challenged Americans to do something about the quarter of our nation living in poverty. The book prompted President Johnson and Congress to pass Medicaid and Medicare. Many books followed that covered these same themes: there is a need for economic justice and as individuals we can do something about it, but expect that our efforts will be opposed by those who benefit from the status quo.

Books are the earth from which movements grow. They feed the imagination, invite reflection, and provoke discussions. In becoming an active citizen, familiarize yourself with the books that are shaping popular opinions in order to better understand how to interweave your message with them. And read books that are also critical of the status quo in order to deepen your understanding of how things can be improved.

Magazines

Magazines carry the same themes found in books but in a more timely fashion. However, their influence has sharply declined over the past three decades. Not only have mainstream magazines like *Time* and *Newsweek* shriveled or disappeared, but alternative political ones have lost their influence as well. However, they are good for keeping a constituency informed about a particular topic or point of view. Nevertheless, magazines are rarely effective in uniting the public around current issues.

Pamphlets

There was a time when pamphlets were the main method of distributing dissenting views, like Thomas Paine's forty-eight-page *Common Sense*, which helped ignite the American Revolution. Toward the end of the heyday of pamphlets, SDS produced over fifty different pamphlets and distributed over one hundred thousand of its *Port Huron Statement*, which promoted its philosophy of participatory democracy, on college campuses. With the advent of social media and blog posts, pamphlets have largely been relegated to the folding tables erected by far right and far left groups at their sectarian events.

Handouts

Handouts are the least expensive print media, and while not as cheap as blasting out e-mails, they are a much more personal medium for delivering a message. Politicians still walk around their neighborhoods knocking on doors and handing out their literature to whomever is home. Chip Marshall, a leading Seattle radical in the seventies, ran for the city council and initiated an innovative use of handouts. Marshall would board a bus and walk down the aisle passing out little campaign cards addressing transportation and other services needed. He exited at the next stop and then rode the following bus to repeat the process. The media loved it, and soon he was on TV and in the newspapers.

I thought back on that experience and realized that by distributing small cards, I could inform workers of their right to receive paid sick leave and protection against wage theft through laws that the city council had recently passed. When I ran for reelection in 2013, I had campaign handouts the size of business cards printed up, saying in bold type, "Working hours you're not paid for? It's against the law. If you're not being paid, call . . ." On the other side it said, "YOU now have paid sick leave. If you're not receiving it, call . . ." At the bottom were my name and my campaign website. I distributed the cards to my supporters, including union members, and we all left the cards behind with our signed credit card payments in restaurants. I was using campaign money not to promote my candidacy but to educate workers of their legal rights.

Posters

Posters are the oldest form of print media for informing the public and calling them to action. They are as effective at promoting social change as ever, because they often have no more than just a few words, an image, or a symbol, like the now universally recognized peace symbol. Even a poster's typeface conveys a cultural message as much as a political one. The sixties' unique swirly typography presented "Make Love Not War" in a manner that invited one's imagination to envision something other than the horrors of war.

Posters can also be seen as a nuisance. The City of Seattle banned posters on telephone poles and started to remove them in 1999 just after I joined the city council. Neighborhood businesses complained that the poles, plastered with overlapping posters announcing concerts and bands playing at local venues, were eyesores that hurt their businesses. The music community joined the ACLU in fighting the ban on the grounds that it limited free speech. The state appeals court agreed and overruled the ban in 2002, saying that the City could regulate the time, place, and manner of temporary signs but could not ban posters from the poles outright.

In response, Mayor Greg Nickels proposed regulations that followed the court's guidelines, and once again anyone walking down the street could find out where local bands were playing. Businesses did have legitimate concerns, but a functioning democracy finds solutions that both accommodate commerce and protect the public's freedom of speech.

Occupy Wall Street's slogan, "We are the 99 percent," rallied many working people around the need for change; nationally, posters displayed the succinct and catchy phrase that heralded the revolt against the corrupt practices of banks. From 1979 to 2007, the average net income of the top 1 percent had grown by 275 percent, while the rest of us in the 99 percent have seen growth averaging less than 60 percent. The 99 percent icon became such a strong symbol of this nation's wealth gap that no explanation was needed, and it fit perfectly on posters that supporters could carry in a march or display in their apartment windows.

One significant poster emerged in Seattle's fall 2013 city elections: "$15 NOW." The general public had already heard the chant "fifteen now" at rallies around the city. The visual image of crowds waving "$15 NOW" posters played a significant role in conveying to the mayor and the city council the demands of fast-food and restaurant workers to raise the minimum wage to fifteen dollars per hour. In the digital age, the simple poster is still a powerful organizing tool.

Newspapers

Daily print newspapers have been dying for a long time. In just the past decade, from 2004 to 2014, the percentage of people reading a newspaper from the previous day has gone from 41 percent to 23 percent. Still, 53 percent of adult Twitter users read one during the week. Reading short 140-character messages is not the same as holding a newspaper and scanning its broad pages displaying multiple titles and pictures. While electronic media is better suited for quickly distributing breaking news to many people, a tiny screen or even a single computer window does not invite the eye to leisurely explore a mosaic of information. Newspapers will be around for a while, and surveys show that much, if not most, of the news distributed on the web, TV, or the radio originated in the print media.

In using a newspaper to reach a broad audience, keep two things in mind: know the paper's readership and get to know the journalists. There are three major types of print newspapers: dailies, weeklies, and campus papers. Dailies have a disproportionately wealthy, white readership compared to the demographics of the general public. The same is true for their newsroom workforce. While the minority population in the country is at 37 percent, the percentage of minorities working in newsrooms has hovered between 12 and 14 percent since 2002. Consequently dailies overall are more conservative than weeklies and campus papers.

Do not rely on influencing a paper's editorial board. They will be cautious at best to support anything that challenges those who benefit from the status quo. It is much better to reach out to select reporters and columnists. Certainly send out a press release, but chances are it will be ignored unless it involves a breaking news story. However, it is important to seek out reporters and take the time to get to know them. Ask them where they have worked, where they went to school, and what their future plans are. Remember that they are workers; they have a job. Make it as easy as possible for them to do their job, and they will be grateful. But never forget that reporters are not your friends; they are journalists, and they are always searching for a potential story, even one you may not want them to tell.

Sometimes, reporters have the theme of their story in their head; they just need you to fill in the blanks. If you give them the right quote, they'll use it. You could talk for an hour, providing all kinds of information and insights, but if they don't need it, don't expect to see a word of what you said in their article. The best you can hope for is that they've taken good notes and might use the information in their next article, which I've found happens about 10 percent of the time.

Columnists have the freedom to devote all of their copy to one topic. Your goal is to provide them with something that catches their interest so that they can comment on it. Review their past columns to acquire a sense of how they approach problems and what topics they tend to circle back to. If you do not know them already, send a complimentary e-mail to them on one of their pieces. Getting in to see them may be rough, but try arranging a quick coffee or beer to find out more about them.

Do not be afraid to talk one-on-one with columnists or reporters who have been critical of you or your issue. Allow them to express themselves, and try to uncover where they are coming from. Push back but don't argue; you are not going to change their mind, but you may be able to soften their stance, and that should be your goal.

In dealing with weeklies, the same strategies apply to working with their reporters and columnists, whether the weekly is a neighborhood paper or a citywide alternative news type. While the content of your message is what motivates you, a writer at a weekly is more likely to talk to you informally based on your personality than your issue.

Many, if not most, weeklies don't endorse candidates or ballot issues. Those that do, even with a smaller readership than daily newspapers, can be very effective because their readers may be more loyal to them and trusting of their opinions. Seek their support as a way to overcome the giant dailies ignoring your issue or being hostile toward it.

When I first ran for the Seattle City Council, both dailies, the *Seattle Times* and the *Post-Intelligencer*, endorsed my opponent. In the previous 128 city council elections, only two candidates had won when both dailies endorsed their opponent. The odds didn't look good. But I succeeded in securing the endorsement of both of the alternative weeklies and a few neighborhood papers, with a combined circulation almost equal to one of the two dailies' Sunday edition. I like to think that my message of investing the City's resources in all neighborhoods and not concentrating them in just a few appealed to the alternative weeklies' young renters and the community papers' older homeowners.

Campus newspapers are the training ground for journalists and the entryway for many students to begin following political and social movements. Generation Progress, funded by the Center for American Progress, has promoted independent and progressive journalism by lending financial support, staff training, and mentoring to campus publications. Their presence helps college newspapers maintain their independence from university administrators who wish to influence the editorial policies of those papers.

Radio

With 11,000 commercial radio stations nationwide, in comparison to 1,400 commercial TV stations and 1,500 daily newspapers, radio would seem to offer the most options for distributing information to the public. However, only 11 percent of radio stations are news or talk stations, with the right wing dominating talk radio programs. For instance, according to Nielsen ratings, National Public Radio, a news station covering many topics, has 26 million listeners, while just Rush Limbaugh, whose talk show is the most popular, has 15 million listeners to listen to him cover any issue of his choosing and Sean Hannity, another conservative libertarian, is in second place with around 14 million.

Radio news reporters and talk show producers often pick up breaking stories from newspapers, be they print or web posts. Given that all-news stations need to have a continuous stream of new information to deliver to their listeners, issue press releases that provide updates on particular situations. If your press release turns the situation in a different direction or contradicts statements that others have made, there is a greater chance that you will be called and interviewed.

Appearing on right-wing talk shows can be risky. Before deciding, listen to some of their prior programs on the Internet. It is critical that they do not interrupt and shout at their guests. If they don't, then I accept the invitation, because at least my message gets out. Also, many of the right-wing hosts are libertarians who are at times critical of corporations as well as government. I was surprised to find them receptive to my opposition of publicly funding professional sports stadiums; both sides saw it as a waste of public funds. So if the host has a libertarian slant, emphasize that government should take care of a city's basic needs before diverting funds to corporate needs.

TV

While the radio may be playing much of the day at work or home, television has remained the public's top daily news source. However, TV news typically reports headlines with little or no analysis, since the median length of a news story on local television, according to Pew Research, is forty-one seconds. And if there is no video for a story, the time goes down to twenty-two seconds.

When thinking of how to get your message covered by the local evening news program, don't count on TV conveying much more than what can be captured on a poster. Plan on delivering a clear message accompanied with a simple visible image. Here are two examples of press conferences that attracted good TV coverage because they adhered to these principles.

Neighborhood activists pushing for more infrastructure investments found, after dusting off and reading through the City's capital investment plans, that money to replace the

Magnolia Bridge had been withdrawn. It was and still is the only bridge that links the Magnolia neighborhood to Seattle's central business district and waterfront. It was rated as being in very poor shape and prone to collapse if there was an earthquake of a magnitude to be expected in the not-too-distant future. We gathered a dozen neighborhood folks under the bridge, pointed up, and said to the reporters present, say your prayers; it could collapse on you at any time. The camera crews loved the visuals. In turn, the City did make critical repairs to the bridge.

The other press conference occurred on one of the city's busiest corners for pedestrian traffic, right outside a McDonald's. A small podium was set up on the sidewalk for a few speakers. We did not block the sidewalk, so pedestrians passed by freely. However, some folks did stop and gather around to listen to our pitch that the city council should pass the fifteen-dollar-an-hour minimum wage. The cameras had a visual feast of people entering and exiting McDonald's, while outside some workers talked about their poor working conditions in the fast-food industry.

Both of these events exemplified the use of free media, in that the activists relied on their own ingenuity to attract media to broadcast their message to the public. But as was noted, your story will not get much airtime, so make your message punchy and timely.

Another option is to take your message to TV channels that have a very well-defined market, like those that appeal to a non-English-speaking audience. One such market is the Hispanic community that Univision reaches. It's the fifth-largest network in the United States, and a larger percentage of their viewers actually watch TV while it's on compared to the other four major networks. When I found that many of the workers in the fast-food industry were non-English-speaking Hispanic workers, I ran ads for my 2013 reelection campaign on Univision. A Spanish-speaking worker speaking directly to the TV audience told how his fellow workers should report violations of the recently passed wage theft law to the City, and the contact number was shown on the screen.

Advertising on broadcast channels is not cheap. It would have taken $150,000 per week for such an ad to be noticed. But I was able to buy 150 spots on Univision for $5,000 and reach those who needed to hear about how their labor rights could be enforced.

E-mail

We all receive e-mails from friends and spammers. But activists should think of e-mails as the most powerful tool for organizing a community, as they can deliver information in a timely and inexpensive manner. I have slowly built a list of contacts whom I send information on current political topics through my e-mailed newsletter *Urban Politics*. To avoid being intrusive, I have first-time recipients confirm that they wish to receive it and they can easily unsubscribe.

I began the newsletter two years before getting on the Council. Since public access to the Internet was limited in 1996, the audience was under three hundred recipients, consisting mostly of reporters, politicians, and community activists. The size of a group receiving your e-mails is not as important as who the subscribers are. Do not treat e-mails as advertisement blasts; treat them as something valuable that you share among friends.

I continue to write *Urban Politics*, and I like to think that I carry on in the tradition of *I. F. Stone's Weekly*, published in the fifties and sixties. Like Stone, I often present critical views on issues that the mainstream media might ignore. My first issue criticized giving a $500,000 revenue-generating garage to the Washington State Convention Center for one dollar a year for thirty years. Although the legislation eventually passed, community and alternative newspapers picked up the story and forced the council to discuss it publicly.

On occasion community newspapers still print or blog *Urban Politics*' content. If you write a good editorial or a research piece, in addition to sending it out to your own list, also send it to the contacts you have made in the media. If editors like it, they will use it. This is particularly true for blogs and smaller community newspapers.

I often use *Urban Politics* to encourage readers to take a course of action or to explain why I took a particular stance on a vote. Political science studies show that politicians can shape voters' opinions by openly explaining their position on an issue. I've often heard constituents say that they appreciate reading why I've voted a certain way even when they disagree with me. To gain the respect of your readers, do not talk down to them. Simply explain the importance of an issue and what your position is on it or why they should care about the issue. Do not try to convince them that you are right or that they would be wrong to think otherwise. With this approach they will be more likely to be receptive of your next message. The long-term goal is to sustain a discussion, not to quickly convert people to your position.

Effective use of e-mail newsletters requires that they be continually updated and sent out with regularity. From managing my own three-thousand-subscriber e-mail list, I've noticed between 5 to 8 percent of e-mail addresses go bad within a six-month period. If you or your volunteers cannot manage your e-mails, use one of the many companies that can; for a minimal price, they can also note which of your e-mails have been opened.

To replenish an e-mail list, collect new e-mail addresses (they're more important than phone numbers) at events you or your group sponsors. Also consider being a co-sponsor of an event, and ask to have access to the sign-in sheet. In Seattle— and this may be true in other cities—the sign-in sheets at city hall public hearings are made available to anyone upon request. If a hearing has attracted a community concerned about an issue, you have a ready-made list available to reach out to. The bottom line is that to keep an e-mail list current, you need a plan for continually adding new e-mail addresses.

Facebook

Using Facebook to reach out to supporters has a distinct advantage over using e-mails because there is no list to maintain. However, since Facebook is continually adjusting its news-feed algorithm in order to maintain profits, most of a Facebook page's fans may not see its updates; Ignite Social Media estimated that the percentage of a page's fans who see any given update was less than 4 percent at the end of 2013.

The continuous stream of information that flows through Facebook posts is actually less accessible than e-mails, because e-mails are tagged with a subject line. A receiver can quickly scan or save incoming e-mails by sender and subject line, a feature that is not currently available on Facebook. Nevertheless, because Facebook is easy to maintain, it can supplement other social media used to disperse information to a broad audience.

Twitter

People got more news from online or mobile devices than from newspapers and radio combined for the first time in 2012. The following year, Twitter, which allows users to post only 140 characters at a time, became the largest social network for providing news to the public. Fifty percent of Twitter users received news from the website, compared to 20 percent of YouTube users and 13 percent of Instagram users. Without a doubt, Twitter, more than any other medium, print or digital, can be a tsunami wave capable of pushing the public to mobilize around political issues.

Twitter can be used to impact local politics. In Seattle, after Socialist Alternative candidate Kshama Sawant was elected to the city council, she made extensive use of Twitter to alert her followers of critical issues. In less than a year, she had about double the number of tweets as the second most active councilmember on Twitter. A person's tweet can have significant outreach if that person's followers retweet the original tweet to their own followers—the more followers, the more retweets. In 2014 the number of followers for each councilmember ranged from a high of Sawant's 7,200 to a low of 2,400. The average number of retweets for councilmembers, exempting Sawant, was thirty-two per month; Sawant's numbers made the others appear to be blacksmiths in comparison to her steel plant rolling out 454 retweets in just one month.

Twitter is just a tool for delivering a message. The content of that message must reside elsewhere. On the Internet that would be either in video or copy format: YouTube or a blog.

YouTube

Like Twitter and Facebook, YouTube is experiencing phenomenal growth, getting over four billion video views a day,

30 percent from the United States. On a local level, activists have used YouTube to share witnessed events, like rallies, demonstrations, and incidents of police brutality. The media has picked up material from YouTube on more than one occasion, forcing the city government to investigate police misconduct. Politicians have also used YouTube videos to deliver political messages, but the trick is to make them visually interesting. Otherwise, they are as dry as stale toast.

YouTube's greatest strength may be its ability to blend culture and politics in a visual format, along the lines of using music and lyrics to deliver a stronger impression than just the printed word. More in-depth political analysis, however, is best found in the blogosphere.

Blogs

Blogs began in the early 1990s as public personal journals posted on the Internet, but in 1996, after the *Drudge Report*, a weekly e-mail dispatch, broke the Monica Lewinsky scandal, blogs began to be seen as news sites as well. Blogs attract visitors in multiple ways: through search engines, e-mails, banner ads, or videos.

Blogs can attract traffic directly when the topic they are writing about is trending high on Google searches. If the topic is hot at that time, then more visitors will be going to that site, because search engines are looking for sites being visited and then place those higher in the list of sites to visit for that topic. For instance, the Economic Opportunity Institute, like most organizations, has a website and a Facebook page. When Patricia Arquette received an Oscar, the story received national attention and was trending. To capture that wave of Internet hits, EOI posted a photo of her and noted that her speech highlighted the importance of equal pay for women.

The other way of receiving visitors is to reach out through e-mails, tweets, or likes on Facebook. A notable example of how people can use a combination of social media to draw visitors to their website is amply seen in how newly elected councilmember Kshama Sawant used them. Her website views numbered 14,830. I was the next closest at 5,560, and the average of all the other councilmembers was less than 2,000 for a six-month period April through September 2014. Sawant's phenomenal lead was due to her using the Internet more frequently than the other councilmembers: she had a third more blog posts than the nearest councilmember, the greatest number of tweets, and by far the highest number of retweets.

Sawant's use of social media helped her obtain 80 percent citywide name recognition after a year on the council, far surpassing all the other councilmembers. In comparison, I had been on the council for seventeen years and had the second-highest use of Twitter and blogs but had only 66 percent name familiarity. Also, when the professional polling firm EMC Research surveyed the popularity of councilmembers, her numbers were higher than all the others but mine, and I beat her by only one point.

It's clear that systematic use of social media made a significant contribution to Sawant's notable achievement in both name recognition and favorable ratings. However, there were two other factors that anyone using social media for political change must also keep in mind. First, having a dedicated following, such as the Socialist Alternative Party in Sawant's case, helps magnify social media's outreach, because followers can direct others to your blog. Second, there should be a clearly understood and consistent message. Sawant's consistency in demanding a fifteen-dollar-an-hour minimum wage resonated with enough of the public to get her elected.

Activist organizations should involve their members in presenting an easily understood message. For OneAmerica, it has been the message "Justice for All." Their website provides in-depth coverage of issues concerning the welfare of immigrants and all ethnic minorities. Google searches bring in about half of their site visitors because of their blog posts; the other half are solicited through Twitter, Facebook, and e-mail blasts using Salsa software. They found that by using hashtags with their tweets, the number of hits on their blog significantly increases if it is a popular topic.

Overall, for blogs to be effective in educating people on an issue, people must be aware that the blog exists. An interlocking network of social media tools that constantly feed each other increases the number of visitors to a blog. When starting a blog, plan how it will fit into the larger Internet community.

CHAPTER 7
PEOPLE TOOLS FOR ORGANIZING

O nce you become aware of how your political environment needs to be changed and you speak out with others for that change, you must still evaluate what tactics are available and which are best for achieving success. Every citizen in a democracy has the right to organize a group of like-minded people to influence their elected representatives. Some, due to wealth or social standing, have more political power than those without similar resources or status. However, smart tactics can overcome the influence of powerful groups.

In politics, the end goal is to write the laws that govern how society operates. Politics play out in two places: outside the arena of government, where citizens can influence government, and inside the arena, where elected officials influence each other to reach a majority vote. The overarching strategies and specific tactics employed in each may differ, but they share the same objective: to determine how political power and public resources are distributed.

Although there are many kinds of tactics that can mobilize the public to push for change, the three methods activists use most commonly are petitioning, polling, and public forums.

Using Petitions

The simplest organizing tool for a citizen to use is the petition. It shows the government, or at times corporations or other institutions, that citizens want it to do something. Not all petitions carry the same weight: it depends who is signing the petition, what is being requested, whether the signatures are verifiable, and how timely it is.

Informal neighborhood petitions, which residents sign to oppose development or up-zoning, are common in cities. I've seen many presented to our city council. They may influence the council's final decision by modifying the proposed change, and that is somewhat satisfying to the petitioners. But I've rarely seen such petitions stop a development. Often that is because the petitions are presented after a developer has had his or her permit approved by the city or the development rights have been legally vested. When it comes to trying to halt a project at that stage, the legislative body will probably not reverse course.

The petitioners then have to decide whether to pursue civil court action based on some procedure that was not followed by either the city or the developer. However, just the threat of a court action can prompt some developers to come to the negotiating table for fear of having a delay in their project cost them too much money.

The Internet has introduced an easier means for petitioning than collecting signatures door-to-door on a sheet of paper. And it can occur on a national or local level. One phenomenal example is the online campaign led by the parents of Trayvon Martin, which gathered more than two million electronic signatures on a website petition within five weeks. Martin, an unarmed black teenager, was shot and killed by a self-appointed vigilante in a gated community in Sanford, Florida. The police questioned the killer, and then he was released without being charged. The family responded, posting a petition on the web urging others to join them in their demand that authorities properly investigate the killing.

While e-mail and web petitions can build national public support around an issue, they are not as effective on the local level. Since signers of electronic petitions can be residents anywhere, local politicians are more likely to discount them, because they need to know the level of constituent interest within their districts. For example, even though e-mails flooded city hall in support of Seattle banning the use of animals in circuses, a poll conducted by a local TV station showed Seattle residents opposed the ban by a 60 to

30 percent margin, with 10 percent not sure. Many European cities had banned circus animals because of poor treatment, but Seattle would have been the first major US city to do so. A majority of the council voted against the ban, in large part because they were not convinced that the e-mails sent supporting the ban were generated locally.

A much more formal and hence more powerful type of petition is one that can force state and local government to take an issue directly to the public for approval. In many states, including Washington, this can be done in two ways: through direct initiative, a process in which citizens draft a proposed law and it then goes on the ballot, or through referendum, which requires that legislation passed by lawmakers be submitted to a public vote. Only twenty-four states allow statewide initiatives, and local initiatives are generally limited to the larger cities in those states.

An advantage of an initiative is that it allows the public an up-or-down vote on a major publicly funded project. When activists raise questions, the proponents of such a project are forced to spend all of their campaign funds defending the public expenditures or the physical impacts on the community. That happened in 1971 when a citizens' initiative ended the Seattle city government's plans to replace 90 percent of the Pike Place Market with offices, hotels, and parking garages. The city council had voted unanimously for the redevelopment plan, both daily newspapers endorsed it, and the federal government offered millions of dollars in urban renewal funds to tear down the old buildings. The redevelopment plan seemed unstoppable. Since lobbying the council and mayor had failed, the only option left was for activists to go directly to the voters with a city initiative.

University of Washington professor of architecture Victor Steinbrueck, working with a group he helped form, Friends of the Market, got the ball rolling to stop the City's proposal. They collected twenty-five thousand signatures in three weeks, forcing the City to put the activists' initiative on the ballot. It was such a popular issue that they only needed volunteers, unlike today, when most initiatives use paid signature gatherers. If an issue has extensive media coverage and a strong simple message that can be delivered to the populace, then you may not need to pay people to collect signatures, particularly if it is a city initiative rather than a state initiative.

Although those opposing the initiative outspent its supporters, the initiative to save the Pike Place Market from developers passed with 75 percent of the vote. The city government finally relented to popular will and pursued preserving the Market rather than demolishing it. Today more than six million people visit the market each year, making it the city's major tourist attraction.

Initiatives can also prompt a government to pursue a project that it otherwise has no interest in. Such was the remarkable case of Seattle's monorail initiative, which would have required the City to build a new forty-mile elevated monorail. It was written in large part by an innovative cab driver, Dick Falkenbury, who collected most of its signatures from petitions placed on unstaffed tables at busy pedestrian intersections. I was the sole city council candidate to endorse the measure, and in 1997, Initiative 41 passed with a 53 percent majority vote. The political establishment was stunned. The day after the vote, Mayor Paul Schell asked me in an off-the-cuff remark, "What were they smoking?" The public ended up approving the $1.2 billion monorail project through subsequent initiatives.

This was a perfect example of an initiative capturing the imagination of the public to do something positive, not just to stop something bad from happening. But the monorail project lacked strong government support. It drifted and failed to deliver a fundable project, finally succumbing to voter rejection on a fifth ballot vote after projected cost overruns dried up popular support. In proposing projects you cannot ignore government's potential role, as you will need its assistance in moving to completion. Without that support it is quite likely that the public will lose faith in it having proper oversight.

Initiatives also have the power to change laws just as Dominic Holden did in spearheading Initiative 75 to decriminalize marijuana. The two youngest councilmembers and I endorsed the initiative. Despite the city attorney's opposition and a visit from the George W. Bush administration's drug czar, John Walters, during which he criticized the measure, the initiative passed with 58 percent of the vote. After a year of enforcement, an evaluation report found that there had been no evident increases in marijuana use among young people, no increase in the level of crime, and no measurable adverse impacts on public health.

These three local initiatives exemplify what studies have shown: initiatives work best when they give political control to local authorities rather than distant ones. In each case, a community was resisting outside authorities—faceless developers, regional transit planners, and the federal government.

Studies also show that citizens tend to favor user fees over tax increases for funding projects. This inclination probably contributed to the success of Initiative 91 in 2006, which restricted $200 million in public funds to build a sports arena for Seattle's professional basketball team, the Sonics. The initiative prohibited Seattle from supporting teams with city tax dollars unless such investments would yield a profit equivalent to the return on a thirty-year US Treasury bond. Mayor Greg Nickels said it went too far, but there was no organized opposition to the measure, and it passed in 2006 with 74 percent voting yes. The team's owners rejected the public's plan and pulled the Sonics out of Seattle, moving the team to Oklahoma.

Initiative petitions must conform to the law, and their provisions cannot interfere with levels of government other than those that are subject to initiative powers. Failure to recognize this limitation has led the courts to nullify initiatives, which happened with two of Seattle's most popular initiatives. In 1978, citizens in Seattle launched an initiative to stop the widening of the I-90 highway into Seattle. After supporters had collected eighteen thousand signatures, a judge ruled that a city law could not override a federal project, and the petition never reached the ballot.

Another instance of a popular initiative quashed by the courts was the effort to stop the county from issuing bonds to pay for a $300 million stadium for the Mariners baseball team. Three individuals played major roles in that campaign: Brian Livingston, who created a neighborhood-oriented populist group called the Civic Foundation, and Chris Van Dyk and Mark Baerwaldt, who started another group, Citizens for More Important Things. I helped form these organizations to bring together liberals and conservatives in opposing the use of public funds for private corporate purposes.

Livingston contacted the media and announced that an initiative to oppose the sale of the stadium bonds would be handed out at the downtown Edgewater Hotel to anyone wanting to gather signatures for it. They expected fifty people to help gather signatures; instead, a thousand people lined up outside eager to help. Within forty-eight hours, they had collected twenty thousand signatures, setting a record. Even though a well-respected attorney wrote the initiative, the courts barred it from going to the ballot because it interfered with the county's ability to issue bonds, a power granted by the state legislature that could not be overruled by a city or county initiative.

Initiatives can be powerful tools for grabbing the government's attention and forcing it to do something. They should also be timely and promote a simple solution to be adopted by the public. Despite their blunt approach, they will be around for a long time to come, since they represent a direct role for citizens to shape public policy.

Using Opinion Polls

Opinion polls are too often overlooked as an activist tool. We tend to think of them as something that is only available to corporations or a well-financed politician. Corporations measure the popularity of their products using polls, and politicians use them to track their own popularity. It would seem that they are too expensive and not relevant to a grassroots effort. That is not true. If used sparingly and strategically, they can influence both the public and politicians.

First consider the cost. A statistically reliable sample needs only a sampling of about three hundred respondents, not a thousand or more. Second, the cost comes in asking multiple questions to reveal the demographic profile of the respondents by each question that they answer. Generally gender, age, residential location, and income bracket are collected. The more questions, the fuller the profile of the respondents. And the more cross tabulations you do for each question by demographic profile, the more people you will need to interview to retain a large enough sample for each response in order to keep your sample reliable. Hence opinion surveys can easily run $20,000, and even an inexpensive one could be $5,000—if you follow the above model. However, you can get a statistically reliable response to a single question for less than $1,000.

The challenge is finding someone to do that, because most companies cannot afford to run a single-question poll. Hence you need to find someone already doing a poll and tag an extra question onto it. I've done this in the past for much less than $1,000.

It may not be as difficult as you think to find a company, group, or person conducting a poll. They are conducted more frequently than you would imagine. A large city is very likely to have a polling company running monthly polls to demonstrate to possible clients what opinion trends are in the market they serve.

Find out who is conducting a poll. See who their owners, officers, and managers are, then look for someone who has an inside connection to the organization. Check that list of company owners and employees to see which have contributed to candidates that might be closely aligned with your issue. Also see if any are on the boards of nonprofit agencies who would be sympathetic to your issue. You can see if a friendly elected official might be running a poll. In other words, you are searching for someone to approach so you can pitch a request to add just one question to his or her poll.

The next question is, what can you do with a single question? The answer is that you can stop a freight train if you want. For example, everyone loves the Olympics, but hosting them in one's hometown is another thing. It was 1998 when the new mayor, Paul Schell, announced that Seattle would bid to host the 2012 Olympics. Like almost everyone else, I thought,

"Why not?" Then I read the agreement that the City would have to sign.

I discovered that the International Olympic Committee required a host city to commit significant governmental resources and to guarantee that the city would cover any financial deficits or lawsuit liabilities arising from the games. In addition, many host cities actually lose money, leading to cuts in local services. Also, site preparation often displaced low-income residents.

My *Urban Politics* e-mail newsletter polled my readership to see if they would support a Seattle Olympics bid knowing that the City of Seattle would be required to provide funding, make up any financial deficit for the games, and cover any law-suits against the sponsoring United States and International Olympic Committees. I received close to a thousand responses representing two-thirds of those e-mailed. The results: 80 percent opposed holding the Olympics, 12 percent were in favor, and the rest were undecided. The media didn't pay much attention to this poll; it wasn't scientific, and it was a poll of a politician's mailing list, not exactly an impartial sampling of the public.

But I thought that it might actually have represented a broader public opinion. If you are going to conduct a poll, first check with your own community members on how they feel about an issue so you know if the road you are heading down has support from your base. I followed up my own poll by approaching a small polling company that did regular professional scientific polls for the media and various organizations. Since they had no additional work to do, they agreed to roll in one question for a minimal cost. It asked whether respondents would support holding the Olympic games in Seattle if the State, rather than the City, was the guarantor of the proposed obligations. Even if there was statewide financial support, 51 percent of those polled said that they would not support an Olympics bid; 32 percent said they would, with the balance uncertain. The findings contrasted sharply with an earlier poll conducted for the private Seattle Bid Committee, which was lobbying the city to hold the games. Their survey received an overwhelming 70 percent vote in support of the bid, but they made no mention of the financial obligations.

It was obvious that a possible financial burden greatly influenced the public. And that was only revealed by a poll not paid for by the advocates. The media picked up my poll results because they differed from those of the Seattle Bid Committee's survey and presented an interesting controversy. One inexpensive question blew a hole in a well-financed survey sponsored by some of the biggest business leaders in Seattle. Afterward, I introduced a resolution that stated that the city council would not support an Olympics bid. The resolution passed by an 8–1 vote.

Opinion polls can accurately reflect public opinion, but they capture it only at a single point in time. It is a major tactical error to assume that a specific poll's results will remain constant over time, and this can lead to overconfidence and electoral defeat. This was demonstrated in the unfortunate demise of Initiative 77, commonly referred to as Seattle's "latte tax."

The Early Learning and Care Campaign sponsored an initiative to raise money for preschool programs and continuing education for teachers. It would have added an extra ten cents to the cost of any cappuccino, latte, iced drink, or Americano sold at a café, restaurant, or coffee stand. Early polling in the spring of 2002 showed the measure had a 74 percent favorable rating. However, the mayor and the city council, with the exception of me, opposed it. The council successfully lulled the proponents into delaying the submission of their signatures with the expectation that would give the proponents time to negotiate with the Seattle Metropolitan Chamber of Commerce. They were subsequently stonewalled and had to wait a year before their initiative would come before the voters.

Although a year had passed from the time of the poll, the supporters, assuming victory, didn't do extensive voter turnout or grassroots education to counter charges that their estimates exaggerated the public revenue generated. Small-business complaints that it would force some to close down or lay off workers further eroded public support. On Election Day, the measure lost by more than a two-to-one margin.

Polls can also be used to influence a legislative body on what kind of action to take. If an outside poll shows that their issue is popular, without spending a dime, activists can use that information as a club to force legislative action. Threaten to go to the ballot to pass an initiative that the polls show would be overwhelmingly favored by the public. In Seattle's struggle to adopt a fifteen-dollar-an-hour minimum wage, the high percentage of citizens who supported the increase was used effectively to get the opponents to the table to negotiate.

The threat of placing a city initiative on the ballot played a critical role in pressuring a majority of the Seattle Metropolitan Chamber of Commerce leadership to accept the mayor's proposal to phase in a fifteen-dollar-an-hour minimum wage rather than fight an initiative that could, if passed, impose an immediate effective date. Their fears were not unfounded; later that same year, San Francisco voters passed a fifteen-dollar minimum wage to take effect in three years, rather than Seattle's phased-in approach, which would take three to seven years depending on the size of the business.

Using Public Forums

If you have an issue, say crime in your neighborhood, and you want to draw the attention of the media and public officials, there are a number of ways to do so. You could hold a rally at a street corner where someone has been shot. The media might show up, and you'll have a thirty-second spot on that evening's news on one or two local stations. But there would be no pressure on politicians to follow up. They could wait till the issue dies down. One-time demonstrations should be integrated into a larger plan for getting public officials to support systemic change.

Holding a public forum about an issue is an effective way to grab the attention of the media and build an organization to address it. The community can use a forum to publicly hold politicians accountable. In its purest form, a forum is not run by the government or by some agency under contract to the government. However, if the government is involved, the community should set the meeting's agenda, place, and time; the community, rather than the government, should be shaping the forum's purpose.

Of course, the success of holding a public forum depends on two major elements: having a good number of attendees and having public officials present to either comment or be asked questions. The easiest objective is to educate public officials about a community problem, and the hardest objective is to have the laws changed.

One of the most successful uses of a public forum was Pramila Jayapal's effort to get Seattle to protect immigrants after 9/11 by organizing a town hall forum to bring immigrants to speak before elected officials about their safety concerns; it was attended by over a thousand people. An example of a very small but very effective forum is how the Allied Arts Foundation, a mainstream nonpartisan group, held a forum with a panel, which I sat on, that simply questioned the wisdom of Seattle hosting the Olympics. The forty-three-year-old organization, long a protector of Seattle's historic districts and culture, was concerned about the Olympics' impact on the quality of life of Seattle residents.

The media's accessibility to a forum's site is important, especially if it doesn't involve any particular neighborhood issue and it is not a breaking story. Since the Olympic Games would impact the entire city, the forum was held in the smallish Two Bells Tavern in the Belltown neighborhood. This was a useful venue because it was near the TV stations, so they could more likely fit the forum into their schedule if there were competing assignments. Also, it was better to have a small, informal setting given that there wasn't a coalition of neighborhood groups to bring out their members. Lastly, and most subtly, it was a favorite watering hole for local media reporters. It always helps to hold a press event at a location where reporters can quaff a beer while covering a story.

The forum attracted low-income-housing advocates and environmentalists concerned about the impact on Seattle's infrastructure. The room was packed with newspaper and TV reporters. Shortly afterward, Allied Arts publicly opposed the Olympics being held in Seattle. It was a turning point. Seeing that an established civic group had recommended not hosting the Olympics, the majority of city councilmembers felt more confident taking that position, and they passed legislation to that effect.

Organizers of a public forum should consider bringing in out-of-state experts to add stature to the event in the eyes of public officials and the media. This would probably require picking up the airfare and hotel costs for the speakers. For a cash-strapped community group that may seem beyond their reach, but there are ways of picking up the costs. If this is an issue dealing with working conditions or fair wages, a local union may be willing to help out. Likewise, environmental groups should be approached for financial assistance if you are organizing a forum on an issue that concerns them. Also, an elected official may tap into an office fund if they are sympathetic to the issue. Finally consider approaching a citizens' commission. This last source of possible funding reflects back on what was covered in Chapter 3 on the usefulness of creating and then using city commissions to push for progressive issues.

A good example of how a citizens' commission can be used to support an issue is when Fair Elections Seattle, a citizens' group interested in reducing money's influence on politics, worked with the City's elections commission to cover the costs of two separate forums on publicly funding local elections. The forums were held in the main public library and at the University of Washington. One forum featured speakers from Los Angeles, Portland, and San Francisco discussing how their systems worked. The other forum brought in a University of Wisconsin professor and a lawyer from the Brennan Center for Justice in New York City to address the pros and cons of this issue. Councilmembers were invited to attend, and several of us did. With the increased interest generated by the forums, the city council took up a proposal for providing public matching funds for city council elections. And they subsequently placed a proposal before voters.

Sometimes it is more important to hold a public forum while an issue still has a community's attention than to wait and take time to bring in speakers or set up a detailed program. Violent crime was on the radar of the Lakewood and Seward Park neighborhoods after three people were assaulted, including a man who was stabbed numerous times in a brutal robbery. In response, the Lakewood Seward Park Community Club, in partnership with the Southeast Seattle Crime Prevention Council, hosted an informal public forum to address crimes in their area. Holding a formal gathering was not as important as holding the event as quickly as possible.

The meeting's organizers used both traditional methods, like displaying posters in neighborhood business windows, and the Internet, sending out e-mails through community-maintained lists and using Facebook. Lakewood Seward Park Community Club president Jeannie O'Brien said, in advance of the event, "I would love to see standing-room only at this event." And that is what happened.

A crowd of more than five hundred overflowed from the community club building, leaving many out in the cold February air listening through windows. Bruce Harrell, chair of the council's Public Safety, Civil Rights, and Technology Committee, and I attended. He addressed the crowd, as did the police chief and other police officers. Although no specific city program was formed as a result of the meeting, the police arrested some youths who had been identified as the perpetrators, and crime did noticeably return back to its normal level.

The underlying tactic in all of the above examples of holding public forums to shape public policy was to focus on a particular issue, rally the community to attend, and have public officials present to witness the community's concerns. Holding forums alone will not bring change, but they can mobilize supporters and grab the attention of those who will need to make the changes.

CHAPTER 8
THE SERVANT IN PUBLIC SERVANT

Make Politicians Work for You

Because voters bestow politicians with the authority to make laws, the media more closely scrutinizes their actions than those of ordinary citizens. An activist wants politicians not only to vote a certain way but also to become activists by using the unique means they have as public officials to help mobilize the public. Two of those means are holding public hearings and creating task forces.

One brief example of how a public hearing can halt a mayor's proposed action is when Seattle mayor Greg Nickels intended to consolidate the Seattle Human Rights Commission, the

Seattle Women's Commission, and the Seattle Commission for Sexual Minorities as a budget-saving measure. He reasoned that one commission could cover all of these constituents' concerns, saving the City money by reducing support staff. However, another effect would have been to diminish the influence of the three groups in guiding city policies. Their members were outraged, and they came to me for help. Together we decided that as the chair of the committee with oversight of these commissions, I would hold a public hearing on the mayor's proposal during my committee meeting.

The council chamber was filled with people who testified about how this cost-saving measure would lead directly to a weakening of the City's ability to serve the constituencies of the three commissions. After the hearing, council president Peter Steinbrueck did not submit the mayor's legislation to the council for formal consideration, and there was no objection from either councilmembers or the mayor's office.

When attempting to influence a city council to either pass or kill proposed legislation, convince a committee chair to hold a public hearing on the issue. To influence that person, identify people who would be affected by the legislation or who contributed to or endorsed that politician's last campaign. Have them call, email, or sign a petition requesting a public hearing.

Although criticized as too process oriented, citizen task forces can involve citizens who otherwise might not have had a seat at the table. Encourage politicians to appoint activists to a task force by arguing that it could work to their advantage: they could point out that critics were included and were involved in formulating the policies recommended by the task force.

Joining a task force carries with it a responsibility to participate, but you must recognize that in doing so, the mere fact that you were involved may be used to justify any decision reached, whether or not you agree with that decision. Overall, I tend to support task forces, because they often lead to an opportunity to introduce progressive legislation and provide a platform for addressing the media.

If the final recommendation is not good, a participant can point out its shortcomings to the media. Politicians are aware of that possibility and strive to avoid any vocal dissent that would imply a failure of their task force. You can use the threat of public criticism as leverage to shape the task force's recommendations.

A task force's usefulness is greatly enhanced if there is a specific objective, a specific timeline, and a politician who is willing and able to champion the task force's recommendations. When Mayor Ed Murray created a diverse twenty-four-member task force to propose a plan for increasing the minimum wage to fifteen dollars an hour, he gave it a deadline and a specific objective. I told him it would fail because the subject matter was too large and the gap between the goals of businesses and the unions was too great to reach a compromise. I was wrong. The mayor actively participated in negotiating the differences within the task force, and only three members did not vote for the final recommendation: Seattle Metropolitan Chamber of Commerce president Maud Daudon, Craig Dawson of Retail Lockbox, and city councilmember Kshama Sawant. Seeing that too many changes would open the door to stalling and possibly killing the legislation, I worked with union leadership and advocates to make some specific and limited adjustments, and the council passed the mayor's proposal unanimously.

Another task force played a similar role in ushering through legislation that would, for the first time, register and inspect all residential rental units in Seattle. The City had tried years earlier, only to have the state legislature preempt the City's ability. After court action got the legislature to change the law, Seattle once again considered passing such legislation. However, two strong property-owner associations still opposed it. The council was sympathetic to tenants, but the majority of councilmembers still did not want to take up the issue.

To bring the issue up for consideration, the activists decided that it would be best to first form a task force to show councilmembers how all sides on the issue had made an attempt to reach common ground. Having a task force would counter any attack on the legislation based on it having been conceived through a poor process. Forming a task force also allowed the debate to directly focus on the merits of the proposed legislation, such as providing safe and decent housing for renters.

The task force met fourteen times over more than a year. Nevertheless, it was worth the lengthy process, and the members finally coalesced around a program that both sides could live with. The legislation subsequently passed. Having a political official closely monitor a task force keeps it on track to reach an agreement. That experience reinforced my belief that putting persistent pressure on the participants to reach an agreement is key to having a task force produce results.

Embrace the Critics

Before being elected to the Seattle City Council, I had fought developments that negatively affected neighborhoods or the public in general. Given this history, I knew many of the neighborhood activists who opposed spending public dollars on big downtown projects.

This type of objection found voice through a network of neighborhood activists who opposed a library bond measure in 1994. The activists saw too much money going to the downtown central library and very little to the system's twenty-two neighborhood branches. Some city officials considered them cranks, folks who are never happy with government. While they did not represent the majority of voters, their efforts were enough to stop the bond measure from achieving the 60 percent voter approval it needed to pass.

Four years later, in 1998, the library bond was again put before voters. This time as a councilmember I voiced the concerns that had led to the measure's previous defeat.

The new librarian for the Seattle Public Library, Deborah Jacobs, understood that she needed to reach out to all the neighborhoods and listen to their individual needs. With energy and a commitment to a more responsive library system, Jacobs attended more than a hundred community meetings in three and a half months to discuss the proposed bond issue. She included neighborhood leaders in the planning and oversight of the bond's expenditures, despite a great deal of distrust between city officials and neighborhood activists.

Elected public officials wanted to know if adopting the changes suggested by the opponents of the earlier bond measure would gain their full support for the new one. In turn, the activists wanted guarantees that the neighborhood branches would be upgraded and that any cost overruns on the downtown central library would not affect those upgrades. Because the neighborhood activists had a clear, measurable goal of wanting more financial support for the branch libraries, the City changed the allocation of capital expenditures from the earlier bond issue, giving the downtown central library a smaller share of the pie. At the same time, the pie was expanded from $155 million to $196 million.

Critics also wanted the amount of money allocated to each branch to be specified. City staff argued that this would reduce their flexibility to adjust expenditures if needed. These differences essentially came down to the question of what level of trust the activists had in city government. To link trust and accountability, I suggested that a Citizen Implementation Review Panel (CIRP) be established, with six members appointed by the City Neighborhood Council, whose members are independently elected by neighborhood district councils. To achieve balance, an additional six members would be appointed by the library board, which is independent of city government but whose members are appointed by the mayor and confirmed by the city council.

I worked with citizens to persuade the library board to support this new entity. In particular, I wanted proof of that support and felt that we needed a letter endorsing it from their chair, Betty Jane Narver. After it arrived, the council unanimously passed the legislation and converted the neighborhood opponents of the earlier library bond measure into avid supporters of the new one.

This conversion was accomplished by adopting three clear procedures. First, the dollar amounts committed to each branch library were set out in the resolution, and if the expenditures for any library facility deviated by more than 10 percent, the CIRP had to be consulted. Second, to assure that the funds were fairly distributed across all neighborhoods, half of CIRP's members represented the six geographic regions of the city. Finally, to guarantee open accountability of how the funds were being spent, all expenditures to implement the library's plan would be made available to the public on the Internet and at all branch libraries.

These accommodations were possible because the new mayor, Paul Schell, and the city librarian, Deborah Jacobs, were willing to accept more citizen participation. And just as importantly, they sold the public on the benefits of a great library system and the wisdom of paying for it.

When the bond issue came up for a vote again, the public approved it by close to 70 percent. I believe what led to its success was the unprecedented citizen monitoring of the financing and the creation of an opportunity fund that established a new library in South Park, one of Seattle's poorest neighborhoods, and also expanded space in three other existing branches to meet community needs. Within ten years after the bond vote, the circulation of books and materials nearly doubled. Getting public officials to include citizen critics in the planning and administration of major capital projects can lead to significant victories for the general public.

Nudge, Don't Lecture

The social dynamics inside a political arena are personal. While working to inform and mobilize the public, you must also convince the few who hold political power that they should listen to the many who don't. It may seem illogical, but I have found that the manner in which information is presented is just as important as its content.

When I began organizing dorms as an SDS member, first I made sure to listen to what the students complained about. They didn't complain about the United States bombing Vietnam or how black students were being killed in the South, although those were the issues foremost in my mind. Rather, they talked about how they didn't want to get sent to fight in a jungle, how bad their professors were, and even how they wished they had beer on campus. So I tried to draw a connection between what I thought they should be concerned with and what they actually were concerned with. I explained to them that it came down to who had power. Did they want to have some power to control their own lives? Did they want to know about what options they had to avoid going to Vietnam, to take better classes, or to drink beer on campus?

From those experiences I learned to listen to what the students wanted and to present their desires in a framework that respected them but also opened them up to considering new ideas. I kept that orientation when I ran for student body president and won—on a campus that supported Richard Nixon over Hubert Humphrey three to one. Of course, it helped that I won over a good portion of the fraternity vote, even though my opponent was a fraternity leader, by pushing for beer on campus.

In running the student council, I found that to get legislation passed it was necessary to coax rather than lecture the student councilmembers. The point was not to prove to them that I was right but that we faced common problems that could be resolved through new approaches. For instance, by recognizing male students' fear of being drafted and sent to Vietnam, I got the student council to support bringing the Quakers to campus to provide draft counseling. At the same time, the student council agreed to work with activists to lower the federal voting age to eighteen.

Later, when tuition was being increased, I reached out to students and their parents to oppose the increase and at the same time solicited their support for expanding student power by requiring that a student have a seat on the university's board of trustees. In each instance, the student councilmembers saw that it was in their own interests to support small practical measures. And I saw them as part of the larger agenda of promoting a democracy that encourages its citizens to participate in its decision making.

One of my first activist activities in Seattle was helping to form a coalition to stop banks from redlining poor and black neighborhoods. We marched up to the Bank of America's president's office to demand that the bank alter those policies. They didn't, of course, but we didn't stop there. We then lobbied city council to do something. It was in that later stage that I learned politicians often want to do the right thing, but they either don't know how or are too timid to try. It reminded me of my student council experiences; legislators are offended if they are lectured to and often respond by digging in their heels to preserve the status quo. But if they are offered a leadership role and given credit for getting others to change, then success is more likely.

I used that approach on the city council in helping to pass Seattle's paid sick leave ordinance. The first step in negotiating is to know whom to negotiate with. On a council with eight other members, I had to determine who was approachable, who could influence others by taking a stand, and most importantly, who would commit to a decision. There is nothing more draining than trying to negotiate with someone who claims to be supportive but cannot commit to actually voting for something.

I found the right person in councilmember Tim Burgess. We took a walk around Green Lake at my invitation, and I asked him what it would take to get his vote. He told me and I found it reasonable. Later, I ran it past the advocates of the legislation. They signed off on most of it, and he in turn agreed to their changes. Both wanted to reach an agreement. I then had my critical pivotal vote. All but one of the other councilmembers then supported the amended version.

Without publicly calling out councilmembers who were either opposed or dragging their feet, I made room for them to decide the best course to take. But it was also important that the community kept up the pressure to pass the legislation. The unions in particular made it clear that supporting this legislation was critical for receiving their endorsement for the councilmember's reelection campaigns. As a result, the councilmembers could and rightfully did take credit for passing the strongest paid sick leave ordinance in the nation.

The sweet spot was getting the councilmembers to feel comfortable voting for the legislation. Since Seattle's council is a nonpartisan body, there are no party loyalties to divide councilmembers, so I've found that when, as a group, they are uncomfortable, they tend to vote no. Conversely, when enough councilmembers feel good about voting for something, most will go along with them if they do not have a strong philosophical objection.

"Being Supportive": Is It Real?

Too often citizens leave a politician's office without having secured a specific commitment to vote for the legislation they want to see. On a regular basis I've had citizens tell me that a councilmember was supportive of their position. And often that is true; however, being supportive is not the same as voting for specific legislation. There are so many reasons why someone's support does not lead to an affirmative vote. The most common reason is that the councilmember needs more time to research the issue before making a decision.

A delayed vote is one of the surest ways of seeing legislation disappear or be defeated. When activists were fighting both for paid sick leave and for increasing the minimum wage, the very first comments made by some councilmembers were that they needed more time to study the issue. In both instances, they said they were supportive of accomplishing these changes but would like another six months to bring in outside consultants to advise them. If momentum is building, do not derail it by delaying a vote.

Make your request as specific as possible. If the bill has not been formally submitted yet, try to obtain a draft of the bill.

Review it with the politician before the committee vote. And when you meet with the politician to discuss the legislation, have specific language ready to present as an amendment. Remember, laws shape our world, and words shape the laws. Asking for something without knowing what exact wording you would like to use opens the door to failure.

Once you have decided on the final version, ask if the politician is supportive of it. If so, close the deal by asking him or her to sponsor either the bill or the amendment. Agreeing to sponsor it nails down the politician's commitment. If the answer is no, ask him or her to second it or to be a co-sponsor or secondary sponsor. The actual procedure will vary from city to city, but under traditional parliamentary rules all motions need a second, and having someone second the motion is a critical step. On more than one occasion I've made a motion and did not have a second, so the item could not even be brought forward for a debate in front of the council. If the politician does agree to second or co-sponsor the legislation, you can use that commitment to get another councilmember to sponsor it. It may be easier to get a sponsor this time, because you've already lined up a vote for the legislation.

If a politician refuses to put his or her name down as publicly supporting the legislation, you have not secured that person's vote. At that point, see if the politician will keep you informed of the bill's progress and any changes made to it. This is a minimal ask, and if someone refuses it, his or her support is weak at best.

The above approach is all predicated on the assumption that you can get a meeting with an elected official. If you cannot, then more aggressive actions are called for, such as picketing outside city hall or people's homes. In one instance, homeless people camped out in various councilmembers' yards to get them to recognize the need for secure and legitimate encampments. It got press coverage, but I found that some councilmembers were even less receptive afterward.

Of course, the effect of intrusive protests will vary by how each is executed and how a public official responds. There are examples of how various protests have worked in the next chapter, but the underlying principle here is that while direct actions may be needed to get public officials to take notice of a problem or to get a meeting with them, at some point you will need to sit and negotiate directly with them. The above strategies are presented in that context so that when the meetings do occur, they will result in change.

CHAPTER 9

PROTEST

Assert Yourself

S ometimes the smallest of incidents teaches us that unless we assert ourselves and protest our living or working conditions, we will have to endure them in silence. Protesting is not limited to large demonstrations; it is something more than just attending a rally or walking in a march. Taking an individual action can make a difference in our lives and be as satisfying as participating in a mass demonstration.

When I arrived at college, I was stuck in a small room with two other roommates, Ken and "the Devil." Ken was a perpetually sweating overweight kid from a small town beside Lake Erie. His prolonged deep breathing and odor filled our room. He was, however, kind, generous, and of strong mind in condemning deviants, like the students at Oberlin, the small liberal arts college where the guys dressed in jeans and the girls had "long stringy-ass hair," unlike the permed hairdos of "our" girls at Bowling Green State University, also known as BG.

The Devil was the opposite of Ken. He was a handsome, trim guy from some big city back east. He sold PB and J sandwiches to kids down the hall after sliding them along our dust-covered floor—just for fun. He was dismissive of religion and its trappings, the stuff that churchgoers like Ken and I held dear. I christened him "the Devil," and he relished it.

Our cultures clashed the first night as he landscaped our walls with *Playboy* pinups. Ken, bashfully amused, did not think the pictures were so deviant as to require protest. On the other hand, being a strict Catholic, I was mortified. How could I live with, sleep with, and wake up to these naked girls every day without being in an endless weekly cycle of sinning and going to confession? Recognizing the ridiculous situation I would be in, I finally objected when he started to post the pinups over my bed. That was too much.

The Devil laughed, enjoying my angst. "You'll have to confess to your priest, won't you?"

I was taken aback. Perhaps I would, but I didn't like being bullied. In a one-on-one confrontation, the Devil was superior to either Ken or me. He was quick witted and forceful; even his physical presence dominated our cubicle. There was no higher authority to appeal to. There was just the three of us. I had to see my conflict not as one just between the Devil and me. I had to see the situation as one of group dynamics; even in a very small group, there is strength in numbers.

I needed to get Ken to agree with me on a solution and then demand that the Devil adhere to majority rule. Ken was not invested in the Devil's landscaping; he was just tolerant of it. I saw that as an opening. All I had to do was get him to allow me to control my own space. It wouldn't cost him anything. When the Devil was out of the room, I suggested to Ken that we divide the wall space equally among us. It made sense to him and he agreed. When the Devil returned, I presented him with the new arrangement that Ken and I had agreed to. The Devil relented and removed the photos from my section of the room—Ken was satisfied with keeping the ones posted over his bed.

It was a small victory, which began with a protest and a willingness to reach out to others for help. More importantly, I began to see politics as a means to allow the weak to challenge the more powerful.

Refusing to Get a Divorce

Eastside Catholic School Vice Principal Mark Zmuda found himself faced with a dilemma. "I was told I could either divorce or be fired," Zmuda said. "How could anyone ask someone else to make that kind of choice?"

Washington State started allowing same-sex marriages in November 2012; in the summer of 2013 Zmuda married his partner. When school principal Sister Mary Tracy, who knew that he was gay, found out about his marriage, she told him he could either dissolve his marriage or lose his job.

Zmuda, who had taught and administered in schools for thirteen years, purposefully moved to Washington to teach at Eastside Catholic School based on the school's antidiscrimination policies, which were posted on their website. The school's attorney, Michael Patterson, told the press, "He was an excellent administrator."

Sister Tracy offered to pay the costs of holding a "commitment ceremony" in place of a wedding. It appeared to be a reasonable offer, but Zmuda would have to accept his status as a second-class citizen unable to marry the person he loved. He would also have to break the sanctimony of marriage in violation of his Catholic faith. At the personal cost of jeopardizing his career, he chose to be fired rather than submit to her demand.

Within weeks of his dismissal, there were student sit-ins and protests at Eastside Catholic School, causing the school to close for winter break early. Seattle mayor-elect Ed Murray, a practicing Catholic and a gay man, stood in solidarity with the protestors, saying that Catholic teachings about social justice and family led him to believe that "we must treat everyone as though they are Christ."

Through Twitter, hundreds of students coordinated to walk out of their classes to call for Zmuda's reinstatement, and students at other Catholic schools joined them. More than eighteen thousand people signed a Change.org petition calling for the church to reconsider its stance on same-sex marriage in light of Zmuda's humanity and Christ's message of unconditional love.

What began as a single act of defiance initiated a soul-searching exercise for many students. As one said, "It makes you stop and think about the school." If those students continue as adults to protect the rights of citizens in the face of unfair practices, Zmuda's initial sacrifice will have made the world a better place to live. Ultimately, Zmuda ended up at Mercer Island High School as a vice principal, and Sister Tracy resigned as a result of the backlash.

Raising Your Fist at the Olympic Games

Sometimes an individual's protest is about taking a public stand that challenges our society's values. Silent demonstrations, without breaking the law or even chanting slogans, can be powerful in effecting change.

American sprinters Tommie Smith and John Carlos broke no laws but caught the world's attention when, in a silent gesture, they lowered their heads and raised their black-gloved fists as they stood on the Olympic winners' platform in October 1968 while the US national anthem played. The previous spring Martin Luther King Jr. had been assassinated. King's death immediately mobilized many African American citizens to demonstrate their anger; over a hundred cities experienced riots, and in Washington, DC, over twenty thousand people were involved. But Smith and Carlos's nonverbal visual statement, which Smith later described as a "human rights salute," penetrated the world's TV audiences in a manner that even the riots could not.

Smith and Carlos were American heroes, winning the gold and bronze medals respectively in the men's two-hundred-meter race, with Smith setting a world record. They had nothing to personally gain from such a sensational, yet restrained demonstration. And they did pay for it. The head of the United States Olympic Committee, Avery Brundage, called their stance outrageous, stripped them of their medals, and sent them home, where they received death threats. *Sports Illustrated* headlined the incident "The Black Athlete—A Shameful Story."

But for others, Smith and Carlos were heroes for standing up for those who couldn't stand up for themselves. Even established leaders took pride in their action, such as baseball legend Jackie Robinson. I saw him when he spoke at Bowling Green State University, and a student asked him about Smith and Carlos's demonstration. Robinson was the first black man offered a contract in professional baseball as well as the first black man elected to the National Baseball Hall of Fame, and at that time, he was the vice president of the National Association for the Advancement of Colored People (NAACP). Robinson responded, "When those young men raised their hands in a black power salute, I felt like raising mine, too. I felt great pride. I think they showed tremendous courage."

Their one moment of silence has lived on. In a 2011 speech, Akaash Maharaj, a member of the Canadian Olympic Committee, said that Smith and Carlos "became the living embodiments of Olympic idealism. Ever since, they have been inspirations to generations of athletes like myself, who can only aspire to their example of putting principle before personal interest."

Women in Black

Providing a constant or periodic public presence to display your message, even without chanting or marching, can impact others and force them to think outside conducting their daily chores. For a number of years I had observed a small line of mostly elderly women all dressed in black standing silently without holding signs in front of City Hall. Like many others who passed them by, I began to wonder, why are they here? What is their message?

I discovered that they were part of the Women's Housing, Equality, and Enhancement League (WHEEL) organization, a nonprofit and nonhierarchical group of homeless and formerly homeless women working to end homelessness for women. The group of WHEEL demonstrators were called Women in Black, and they held a silent-hour vigil whenever a homeless person died outside without shelter in King County. From 2000, when they first started, until 2015, they have stood silent for more than five hundred homeless people.

I also learned that Women in Black was an international network of women who stand in silent vigil, calling for peace, justice, and nonviolent solutions to conflict. The group had been standing in vigil at Seattle's downtown Westlake Park once a week for the noon hour every Thursday for years. The simplicity of these protests did not detract from the seriousness of their message nor their power to effect change.

After eleven years of vigils, the Women in Black succeeded in having the Seattle Parks Department work with their Homelessness Remembrance Project to install a large art piece called the *Tree of Life* in Victor Steinbrueck Park as a place to provide comfort and a sense of "home" for homeless people, as well as to promote greater understanding of them. For another project, Leaves of Remembrance, the City installed brass images of leaves on the sidewalks, each one bearing the name of an individual who died while homeless. Perhaps those who gaze upon those leaves give some thought to the homeless who have passed away in the night, outside, alone, and forgotten by society.

Quietly displaying an object to catch a pedestrian's attention can result in that person reflecting on how our society operates and how they can do something about it. Women in Black serves as an example of how it does not take money or masses of people to alter others' consciousness.

Stopping Coal and Oil Trains

The most dramatic type of protest is when individuals face physical danger while trying to stop an action from occurring. The media is certain to appear, conveying the message to a much larger audience than just those present. The commitment and passion of the protestors captures the attention of many who may be uninvolved in or even unaware of a particular issue. The images of people facing possible personal harm for a cause almost demands some curiosity from others. This strategy has drawn attention to the dangers present when trains carrying coal or oil travel through urban areas. And it has opened up the larger conversation about how coal and oil trains contribute to global warming.

In September 2014, five citizens chained themselves to a tripod structure in front of a mile-long oil train trying to leave the Burlington Northern Santa Fe (BNSF) rail yard in Everett, Washington. Similar citizen blockades occurred in other parts of the Northwest: in Montana residents sat on the tracks to block a train, in Portland a woman locked herself to a fifty-five-gallon barrel filled with concrete to block oil trains, and in Anacortes, Washington, three people blocked oil trains at the refinery using a similar tactic.

These actions were in response to the increasing number of trains traveling through urban areas carrying coal and oil from new drilling and mining projects like the Alberta tar sands, Bakken shale oil, and the Powder River Basin. The planned twenty new or expanded coal, oil, and gas terminals high-lighted the potential danger of transporting coal, oil, and volatile gas through dense populations.

In the summer of 2013, a train carrying crude oil derailed and exploded in Lac-Mégantic, Quebec, killing forty-seven people. The following summer in Seattle, a train ran off the tracks passing underneath a major bridge parallel to a highly utilized bike path during the morning rush hour. Three of its one hundred tank cars, carrying the highly flammable and easily ignited Bakken crude oil, were derailed. The BNSF Railway announced afterward that they move eight to sixteen oil trains per week through Seattle, all containing a million or more gallons of Bakken crude oil. According to the US Department of Transportation, areas up to a half mile or more from an accident site are considered vulnerable.

One protestor said, "If elected officials won't stop the fossil fuel takeover, we'll have to do it for them." Councilmember Mike O'Brien listened and led the city council in being the first city government nationwide to call for an immediate end to oil train transport near neighborhoods. However, the protests will continue as long as there is physical danger to communities from oil trains. Those trying to halt global climate change will also continue to disrupt coal trains that ship coal from North America to China, where coal is burned with minimal environmental restrictions.

Without a doubt these protests gained the attention of the media and politicians. However, it is important to use

demonstrations as more than just a means to show that your position is the right one; you must convince others that laws must change.

There must also be public outreach to get legislation passed. Good organizing that attracted 2,500 people to attend a federal-state scoping hearing on this issue in Seattle was a particularly effective way of following up direct actions that stopped coal and oil trains.

Occupy Wall Street

In November 2011, I found myself possibly facing an Occupy Wall Street action at a town hall meeting. I had been invited to moderate a panel to discuss the relevance of the Occupy Wall Street movement. The name derived from a protest encampment that had begun two months earlier at Zuccotti Park in New York City's Wall Street financial district. Local Occupy movements also formed protest encampments in the heart of Seattle, Los Angeles, Oakland, and many other cities.

The evening's event was at Town Hall, a facility run by a non-profit dedicated to providing a public forum on issues of the day. The alternative weekly newspaper the *Stranger* co-sponsored the event. The panel consisted of three members of Occupy from different committees, as well as Nick Hanauer, co-author of *The True Patriot*; Lynne Dodson, secretary-treasurer of the Washington State Labor Council; and Frank Greer, co-founder of Amnesty International. All of the panelists recognized the need to eliminate the growing income gap in the nation. Given the lack of a Republican on the panel, I thought it would be a pretty tame discussion that would lack tension. I was so wrong.

In the green room, where the panelists met for the first time, the three Occupy activists informed the other panelists, me, and the Town Hall coordinator, Bob Redmond, who had arranged the event, that they would not participate on a panel that talked down to the audience. Instead they wanted the entire evening to be converted into an Occupy general assembly where everyone in the audience who wished to speak would use a people's mic, meaning the entire audience would repeat the speaker's words out loud. This method was originally used in New York City when the Occupy encampments were denied the use of electricity to set up a speaker system. The people's mic was born out of necessity, not as a community-building exercise. Nevertheless, those participating in the Occupy encampments had adopted it as customary use in general assembly meetings, and many found it did create a community for them. However, the evening had been organized and publicized as a panel discussion followed by a question-and-answer period, not an Occupy general assembly.

By a show of hands, approximately half of the eight hundred people in the hall considered themselves part of Occupy Seattle, with a third having attended a general assembly. After that, Redmond turned to me and said, "I'm sure glad Nick Licata is moderating this forum and not me." I had a sick feeling in my stomach.

After the panelists briefly introduced themselves, a young woman leaped onto the stage and yelled, "Mic check!"—the signal for half the room to echo her words. Was this a trampling of free speech or an expansion of it to everyone? If it was an attempt at the latter, it was clumsy at best, and at worst, it was a dismissal of others' rights to enjoy an expected evening of an informed discussion by the panelists.

It demonstrated the ability of a cohesive group to lead a crowd by speaking the loudest and drowning out others. A number of the older regular attendees of town hall meetings left after the shout-a-thon process continued. I tried to corral the energy of the Occupy folks within a democratic process and called for a hand vote of the audience to see who wanted to hear the panelists and who wanted to continue with the people's mic assembly. The Occupy people lost the vote but shouted down the decision by demanding that there had not been enough time to discuss and explain what a general assembly was. I recognized that I did not have an alternative group to counter the organized core of Occupy people and that if I tried to push ahead with the panelists' speaking, they would have been repeatedly interrupted. So I agreed to take some time for folks to have their discussion. Afterward we took another tally, counting each hand raised, and the panel approach won by an even larger margin than the first vote.

While I managed to avoid a collapse of the evening's event, I spent an hour in that effort before the patient panelists finally began their presentations. Community college student

JM Wong epitomized the activists' euphoric message; they were part of a radical collective that was too big to fail, and workplaces should be run as general assemblies. Another activist panelist, Tabitha Montesory, a preschool assistant teacher, found that the Occupy encampment provided her with close relationships and friendships for dealing with society's illnesses. The audience was sympathetic, but when the non-Occupy panelists talked, they were booed or shouted at from time to time. Still, despite intermittent interruptions, the panelists were not completely prevented from talking.

When the video of the event was posted, there were a record 262 comments posted on the *Stranger*'s SLOG website. Most were critical of Occupy's insistence on trying to convert that evening's meeting into an Occupy general assembly. A sixty-nine-year-old woman quoted in the *Stranger* captured the drift of many commenters: "I'm turned off by the negative shouts, repetition, and all I can think about is a cult. And I believe in every one of their damn principles."

That incident was not part of a larger Occupy plan to disrupt public dialogues. Instead, it was most likely a passionate appeal by the activists to the audience to embrace a new way of thinking. The activists clearly did not succeed, in part, I believe, because they could not articulate a few simple executable objectives that could be carried out through the existing democratic political system. Democrats would have welcomed them. A local Democratic Party leader, Chad Lupkes, posted that he hoped that the Occupy movement would work to replace those elected officials, including Democrats, who were not acting in the interest of the 99 percent.

The Occupy movement instead pursued a multitude of issues, and as time went by the remaining core of those occupying encampments leaned more toward overthrowing capitalism than reforming the current political system. Its support, according to an NBC and *Wall Street Journal* poll, fell by over half six months after New York City shut down the Occupy Wall Street encampment at Zuccotti Park. Only 16 percent of Americans still supported the movement by the spring of 2012.

Professor Todd Gitlin, a former SDS president, asked where Occupy's leaderless revolutionaries went. His answer: they dispersed into several left-wing-issue campaigns. Some efforts, like Strike Debt, which opposed "debt because it is an instrument of exploitation and political domination," made a significant impact. By the end of 2013 it had succeeded in erasing $13.5 million of medical debt for close to three thousand individuals by raising funds to purchase debt for a fraction of its face value. Other Occupy objectives, like bank reforms and public funding of campaigns, also came to fruition when politicians pursued them. Some of the larger cities, like Seattle, passed legislation requiring banks with city deposits to do social equity investments.

Nevertheless, the Occupy movement faded as a unified political force, while the Tea Party movement focused on gaining political power. John Wellington Ennis, documentary filmmaker of *Pay 2 Play*, would say that is an unfair comparison, since Occupy was a protest, not a political party. He points out that the Occupy movement "viewed officeholders as courtesans for the corporate class" and hence rejected electoral politics, while "the Tea Party turned outrage at the government into electoral gains," admittedly with the help of corporate money. The bottom line is that the Occupy movement rejected working within the Democratic Party, while the Tea Party chose to work within the Republican Party—and take it over.

The Tea Party Crashes the Party

The Tea Party movement exemplifies how money can feed and steer the course of a rebellion against the establishment to, in fact, bolster the status quo. It also serves as an example to activists of how protestors can gain political power through entering electoral politics.

President Barack Obama's stimulus act became law in February 2009 with only three Republicans in all of Congress voting for it. The act provided public funds for infrastructure, education, health, and energy, while also giving federal tax incentives and expanding unemployment benefits. It relied on government intervention to turn the country's deep recession around, a solution that flew in the face of the libertarian antigovernment philosophy of those who believed that only free-market solutions could address the nation's recession. Right-wing talk radio lambasted Obama and spurred its millions of listeners to attack him, the Democratic Party, and government in general.

The Tea Party movement began in the early spring of 2009 with nationwide protests against taxes. With employment the lowest in over sixty years, anger filled the air at a government that was seemingly adding to their economic burden. White middle-class men, who either had lost their jobs or feared losing them, provided the ground troops. A 2012 CBS News and *New York Times* survey of self-identified Tea Party supporters revealed that 89 percent were white and just 1 percent were black. The Occupy movement was born from similar economic frustrations at the end of 2011, although their active base was youths being stuck in low-wage jobs.

The Tea Party activists, just like the Occupy activists, rejected a hierarchical organizational structure, instead spawning at least a dozen Tea Party–affiliated organizations. However, unlike the Occupy movement, which also splintered into many different organizations, corporations saw that this movement aligned with their interest in keeping taxes low and stepped up to finance the Tea Party organizations.

Two major right-wing pro-Republican foundations did the initial financial heavy lifting: Americans for Prosperity and FreedomWorks, the first openly funded by David Koch and family, owners of the largest privately held energy company in the country. They jumped on the bandwagon early, providing money and access to their combined three-million-people membership. They also provided an intellectual justification for the movement when Dick Armey and Matt Kibbe, the president of FreedomWorks, released their best seller, *Give Us Liberty: A Tea Party Manifesto*. This demonstrates how books, as an old print technology in the digital age, still play a major role in propagandizing a movement's philosophy to a broader audience.

Although the Tea Party activists were proudly independent of the major political parties, as were the Occupy activists, their political and financial backers were die-hard conservative Republicans. In the summer of 2009, Tea Party members received instructions from members of the Republican Party on how to disrupt the town hall meetings hosted by Democratic members of Congress. Unlike the experience that I had with the Occupy activists, this was a well-planned attack, not just in one location but across the nation.

A leaked memo from FreedomWorks' Tea Party Patriots outlined the tactics to be used at these events. "You need to rock-the-boat early in the Rep's presentation. Watch for an opportunity to yell out and challenge the Rep's statements early. The goal is to rattle him, get him off his prepared script and agenda. If he says something outrageous, stand up and shout out and sit right back down. Look for these opportunities before he even takes questions." Other approaches were more direct, like when eighty-three-year-old representative John D. Dingell was shouted down at a community meeting by foes of Obama's health-care overhaul calling out, "Shame on you!"

For a group that championed freedom, to shout down the opposition seemed ironic. However, the Fox News Network covered Tea Party events and their intimidating actions at others' events favorably. Stephen Burgard, director of Northeastern University's School of Journalism, said, "Fox appears to be promoting these events at the same time it is presenting them in a way that looks like reporting." With good funding and sympathetic TV coverage, the Tea Party began to influence the public.

By the end of the summer of 2009, a *Wall Street Journal* and NBC News poll found that over 40 percent of those interviewed looked on the Tea Party movement favorably. Their ratings peaked when 60 percent of Republicans and GOP-leaning independents classified themselves as supporters of the Tea Party in November 2010. The movement helped Republicans take control of the House of Representatives that year. FreedomWorks alone spent over $10 million on the 2010 elections. And they were still using tactics that had been employed the prior year in harassing Democrats at community meetings. Their new employees were required to read Saul Alinsky, the left-wing community organizer who advised using disruptive tactics from time to time.

Two years later in 2012, twenty-seven new Tea Party conservatives were elected to the House, with the Senate seeing three new Tea Party members. By January 2013, the Tea Party Caucus included 48 members out of the 435 representatives. The following year Eric Cantor, the number-two

House Republican leader, was defeated by a Tea Party member for reelection because Cantor was too close to Wall Street. That fall Louisiana representative Steve Scalise, a Tea Party supporter, became the House majority whip. As a former state representative, he voted against creating a holiday to honor Dr. Martin Luther King Jr. in both 1999 and 2004. With these gains in the Republican Party, the Tea Party took on a dominating role in the party, despite their support slipping to only 20 percent in public opinion polls, according to an AP-GfK survey taken in March 2014.

It is obvious that corporate money made the Tea Party's political success possible. But there was another factor in play as well. They focused on gaining political power and not on organizing in the streets. Instead of expending energy on sustaining tent encampments and fighting the authorities from shutting them down, they aimed to gain control of Congress.

The Occupy movement did not systematically try to influence the Democratic Party from within. The Tea Party, on the other hand, challenged incumbent Republicans for seats in Congress. And then they worked to turn out the vote. In other words, they converted their protest from being symbolic and generalized to being practical and specific.

As a result, by 2015, they were helping shape national policy within Congress. Meanwhile the Occupy movement had far fewer supporters in Congress. The Tea Party protest movement had gone from being opposed to those in power to becoming those in power. Whether they can sustain that status or not, they succeeded in redirecting the Republican Party toward a greatly more conservative agenda committed to reducing the size of government and its ability to provide services to all citizens.

The lesson for all activists is that you need to have a dual-prong approach to changing the political landscape: being in the streets protesting arouses the public, but afterward quiet organized efforts are needed to get your supporters elected to office so that they can actually change the laws.

CHAPTER 10
DISRUPT THE CULTURE

Disrupt the Status Quo, Gently

One of the biggest hurdles citizens face in convincing others to challenge the status quo is the culture that frames our daily expectations. While some of us are born rebels, most of us accept what we have grown up knowing. It's a comfortable culture of continuing the past without questioning the assumptions that sustain it.

To open up minds to new possibilities it may be necessary to gently jar people out of their daily routines in order to show them that their life will go on and no disaster will result. This strategy arose in the sixties, exemplified by events such as

"Gentle Thursdays," which were invented at the University of Texas at Austin by the underground newspaper the *Rag* and the local chapter of SDS.

The basic concept was to encourage students to expand their perceptions of what is possible. They held outdoor events open to everyone, with the express purpose of breaking down ideological, social, and cultural differences. Students were encouraged to do something that they might not normally do, like have a picnic on the campus mall, carry balloons, play music, read poetry, share flowers, and draw with chalk on the sidewalk. The organizers hoped that these harmless activities released the spontaneity that dwelt inside each student but that they did not have an opportunity to express.

The idea spread to Bowling Green. Our SDS chapter sponsored a Gentle Thursday, and even with minimal prior organizing more than two hundred students showed up. We supplied the chalk, and soon the campus's main walkway was covered with colorful swirling patterns and flowers. The police arrived, expecting a protest, and instead were bemused, as were the hundreds of other students who lined the sidewalk, gawking at the chalk art while respectfully walking around it. The *BG News* ran a photo with a caption saying that someone had called the event a "Happening," a term that had spread around the nation and that described any burst of imaginative activity that was different, unexpected, and celebratory of life.

In the spring of 1967, an open-air gala celebrating life, held in San Francisco, was referred to as a Happening. Soon afterward, on a warm Easter Sunday, activists in New York held their own "Be-In" with some twenty thousand people gathering on Sheep Meadow in Central Park. *New Left Notes* described it as "an unstructured affirmation of life by the City's hippie, arty, radical and exuberant people, who danced in circles, flew kites, kissed and embraced, took bites out of a cake, roasted marshmallows, gave away bread, read poetry and exercised their dogs." At one point, two officers were surrounded by a crowd charging at them chanting "love, love, love." In response, the police released the safety catches on their guns, but amiably held their fire.

All of these events offered, in some small way, the freedom to do something that was a break from daily routines. In doing so, perhaps the participants would begin to think of the future as something malleable to their will, something they could actually influence. In the summer of 1967, the goal was to promote love over war, and today the same challenge exists in spurring people to be more flexible in considering what they can do with their lives. And what better way to open those doors than through having fun?

The massive Happenings of that era were decades ahead of management practices in recognizing that breaking everyday behavioral patterns is at the heart of getting people to think differently. When scholars began to recognize and measure the creativity of workers, they concluded that work environments with rigid rules, checks, and controls inhibit creativity. Their solution was for companies to make room for play as a way to release their employees' imaginations and to sustain innovation. Microsoft, Google, Amazon, and similar companies, as well as some universities, adopted this approach.

Northeastern University, a private nonprofit research university, opened a branch in Seattle in 2013 that offers graduate classes in computer science and other fields relevant to the region's high-tech industries. At their open house, I discovered that they had a Ping-Pong table on each floor. I asked the CEO, Tayloe Washburn, why he had set them up. He replied that this simple, low-energy activity improved thought processes and sparked innovation. The tables also provided a way for staff, faculty, and students to interact in a nonhierarchical environment.

Since City Hall already was hosting public concerts and rallies, I thought we should add a public Ping-Pong table to the mix. I suggested that if Northeastern would donate one to the City, I would put the university's logo on it and make the table available to the public for free, even providing paddles and balls. In response, Washburn sold a table to the City for one dollar, and in August 2013, the table was set up and available for use in the City Hall, making it perhaps the only city hall in the nation to have a public Ping-Pong table in its lobby. I found that it attracted workers from nearby office buildings.

In the spirit of Ping-Pong diplomacy, I even invited Dori Monson, a local conservative radio talk show host and steady critic of mine, to play me in a game. He came, and he won. Nevertheless, the game demonstrated that the simple addition of a Ping-Pong table created a social node that could bring together many types of people, creating a broader sense of community. And the City started installing free Ping-Pong tables in some of its parks after crime incidents decreased in the first park to receive one.

All of these efforts, from Gentle Thursdays to Ping-Pong tables, share a key element for organizing people: they offer an environment with greater social freedom and more opportunities to interact with other people around a shared activity. Providing space and time for people to exchange ideas and talk about common interests and experiences creates a fertile ground for questioning the status quo and creating new communities, much like my college friend Ivan had initiated for me.

Explore New Cultural Values: Start an Intentional Community

Building strong social networks through intentional communities can change established cultural values. Having an accessible place to meet, whether in a formal or informal setting, is critical to exchanging ideas and challenging oppressive values that limit human growth.

When neighborhood activists supported a new library bond measure to refurbish old library buildings or erect new ones, they insisted that each building have a community meeting room, a place where their community councils or any other local group could meet outside of their homes. Gathering places are critical to organizing communities of interest.

Taverns served as gathering spots for organizing the American Revolution. The tradition continues today. The national Drinking Liberally discussion group has close to two hundred chapters across the country that meet in taverns to plot a liberal future for the country.

Aside from libraries and taverns, the ideal place for gatherings is someone's home, because such events can be less public and formal, allowing for more serendipitous discussions. Unfortunately, large gatherings in homes are not common, given that most houses cannot accommodate them. However, collective households renting, or even owning, larger houses can nourish emerging new communities.

One collective household, dedicated to promoting community and environmental issues, has sustained itself in a three-story, thirty-six-room mansion in Seattle since 1972. A group of twenty students, their friends, and two married professors with their wives and children moved in after putting down $5,000 and buying the house for $45,000 during a recession when no one else wanted it. The group captured the flippant spirit of the day by naming their new abode PRAG (Provisional Revolutionary Action Group) House. I moved in two years later with my then girlfriend, Nora Leech, stayed for twenty-five years, and raised our daughter there. PRAG has remained a residential collective, becoming part of the nonprofit Evergreen Land Trust (ELT).

By providing a meeting place to build friendships around common causes, PRAG gatherings produced a number of community-based projects. One of the first was the Northwest Tilth Association, a network of counterculture environmentalists and food activists. They laid the groundwork for generating an organic-food economy in the Northwest.

Other projects followed, like the annual dance marathon called Give Peace a Dance, which raised more than $500,000 to stop the escalating nuclear arms race raging between the United States and the Soviet Union in the late 1980s. Aside from raising funds, it created a larger community by linking thousands of people around shared political beliefs. Overall, in holding over a hundred social gatherings at PRAG House, I discovered that by throwing parties around a political theme, you could have fun and build social networks for change.

As Seattle prospered, large old houses like PRAG became unaffordable to students and low-wage workers, who often had to settle for living in small studios. With more than half of the city's housing in multiunit residential buildings, Seattle became the US city with the third-highest rate of people living alone, with few homes available for intentional communities.

Nevertheless, a few collective households have come into existence, but their residents rent, rather than own, their homes. As a result, an owner could sell the building at any time, destroying the community. The InArtsNW co-op, a group of over twenty individual artists, rented a house similar in size to PRAG House in an adjacent neighborhood for over six years. When threatened with eviction in 2015 because the house was up for sale, the co-op explored joining a residential land trust like the Evergreen Land Trust. By donating the property to a nonprofit land trust, the owner could receive a tax credit to offset other income. That is how the ELT had acquired other houses.

Another model for securing a permanent residence for an intentional community is to remodel an older building through government assistance. Cathryn Vandenbrink, an artist who was displaced from her rental unit, worked with her Pioneer Square neighborhood organization to convert an old commercial building into the affordable Tashiro Kaplan Artists Lofts for low-income artists, musicians, writers, actors, and their families to live and work. Previously another building serving over a hundred work-live artist spaces in that neighborhood had been converted to high-price condos. In response, the neighborhood came together to preserve their artistic community. But the effort was not cheap; it cost $16.5 million from a mix of public funds and private foundation contributions.

With or without outside funding, residential land trusts can provide permanently affordable housing for intentional communities in traditional single-family houses or converted commercial buildings. By requiring our local governments to support regulations and incentives for encouraging these developments, we can cultivate values that sustain cooperation and creativity.

Join a Parade

The effort to change the existing culture doesn't necessarily have to be one of confrontation or even struggle. Instead, you can celebrate a new culture or a culture of activism. Parades are perhaps one of the best ways to encourage those outside a particular movement to recognize the positive elements of that cause. Because parades are intended to be nonconfrontational, organizers most often have sought city permits in Seattle for closing the roads along the parade route. Consider choosing a route that passes by retail establishments so that shoppers find themselves looking at the parade while window-shopping.

If you are organizing a parade, publicize its openness by inviting everyone to join in. Let friends know that participating in parades can be a very personal way to meet new people with similar views as well as a way to publicly demonstrate their beliefs.

If you believe in promoting social justice, try joining one or both of two major celebrations that occur every year in cities across the nation: MLK Day and pride parades. The former celebrates the Reverend Martin Luther King Jr. on the third Monday of January each year and usually includes a march as well as other activities like workshops and volunteer community work. Pride parades, usually held in June, are colorful, festive, and accompanied by other events that celebrate lesbian, gay, bisexual, transgender, and queer (LGBTQ) culture. You don't have to be black or part of the LGBTQ community to participate in either; everyone is welcome at these celebrations.

In 1979, eleven years after Dr. Martin Luther King Jr. was assassinated, Congress considered making King's birthday a national holiday but failed. After overcoming President Ronald Reagan's initial opposition, a federal holiday was established and first observed on January 20, 1986. However, it wasn't until 2000 that all states recognized the day as a paid holiday for state employees.

Seattle, like a number of other cities, did not wait for a federal holiday; we had our first MLK march here in 1982. The MLK Celebration Committee, open to all and chaired by King County councilmember Larry Gossett, runs the annual march, rally, and workshops, the last of which identify local issues facing citizens in King County. In 2014, the event attracted six thousand participants, providing many of them with an opportunity to work with others on a wide variety of political issues, as well as to do community work as part of federal legislation that transformed the holiday into a day of citizen volunteer service in honor of Dr. King. If you get involved in organizing an MLK Day event, emphasize the opportunity to volunteer for community work by notifying local community clubs and church congregations and seeing if they will include that information in their bulletins a month in advance of the march.

Seattle held its first pride parade in 1977, two years after Mayor Wes Uhlman, bowing to intense prodding by the gay community, made the last week in June the official Gay Pride

Week. Many other cities followed Seattle in making the last week of June the official week to celebrate gay pride.

Foes of Uhlman's decision picketed outside City Hall and threatened to recall him because of his supporting Gay Pride Week. While nothing serious came of that, supporters debated whether their event should be a march or a parade. A march lent itself to showing support for a number of other causes, like abortion, labor organizing, or economic reforms. A parade was more in the nature of a celebration of gay visibility through entertainment and music. The struggle came down to local socialists arguing with local businesses on which approach was more effective in supporting the LGBTQ community.

By the late 1980s the transition from marching to parading had been made, and the parade became one of the most attended in the city and the nation, attracting more than three hundred thousand people each year. The political messages are still there, but the entertainment is what draws folks. The lesson learned is to use culture to deliver your message; don't allow your message to overwhelm the culture.

Create a People's Poet Populist

In organizing our fellow citizens to make political or economic changes, we should not ignore the opportunity to include culture as a pathway toward rethinking how the world works around us. Poetry may be the oldest means for conveying new insights on how we relate to our social environment. It can open minds to views that may seem quite dangerous to the status quo.

I saw how the Allen Ginsberg poem "Howl," whose first line began, "I saw the best minds of my generation destroyed by madness," was powerful enough to get its publisher, Lawrence Ferlinghetti, charged with obscenity. The ACLU successfully defended Ferlinghetti by arguing that the First Amendment protected "Howl" because it had "redeeming social importance." Unfortunately, radio stations airing "Howl" in 2007, fifty years after its publication, could be subject to an FCC fine of $325,000 per profane word. The government certainly didn't underestimate the power of poetry.

If you are organizing an event, begin it with a local poet reading an original poem for the occasion. It may not be what people expect. It will announce to all present that anything is possible, even a poetry reading. I began that practice after becoming student body president at Bowling Green State University, when I replaced the student council's chaplain's blessings that began its meetings with a poetry reading. I continued the practice of opening a meeting with a poetry reading when I became a city councilmember. For eighteen years my committee meetings have begun with a local poet reading original material as part of a program called Words' Worth. All of the poems were then posted on my council web page.

Changing the world one poem at a time is possible if you can devise ways to use poetry as active social engagement and not just confine it to words in a book. That opportunity came up when neighborhood-based arts organizations complained that city government focused too much on the major art institutions and ignored the new and emerging ones.

At the suggestion of community art groups, who felt that they were overshadowed by the major art institutions in the city, I worked with them to organize a Seattle Neighborhood Arts Celebration (SNAC) to highlight small neighborhood-based arts organizations. Most of these organizations, while doing interesting creative work in their own communities, were unfamiliar with what other neighborhood arts groups were up to. By familiarizing themselves with their neighbors' activities, community arts groups could then share resources, refine their best practices, and even reduce operational costs.

The first SNAC featured twenty-three poets and performers at Seattle's downtown Benaroya Hall. To highlight the connection that many poets have to their communities, the audience and later the general public voted for their favorite poet. Bernard Harris Jr., a postal employee, became Seattle's first poet populist.

Poet populist elections were held on and off from 1999 to 2009. Unlike traditional poet laureate appointments, in which dignitaries or government officials select a poet, a public vote determined which Seattle resident would be the annual poet populist. The nominees were picked by thirteen Seattle arts and literary organizations to represent the broadest range of talent possible. The poet populist project promoted the idea that arts and civics don't have to be separate.

The winning poet received a cash prize and would write an original poem for inclusion in the City's archives. In addition, he or she would hold public readings at schools and libraries, and often were invited to read at bookstores, colleges, businesses, and at opening ceremonies for new public and private developments. The City of Cambridge, Massachusetts, learned about our poet populist program and created their own.

Unfortunately the program had to be suspended during the Great Recession due to lack of funding. However, in 2013 former Washington State poet laureate Kathleen Flenniken, along with other people working in the literary field, came to the City asking it to resurrect the poet populist program. We expect to begin another era of civic poetry that enlightens our populist consciousness by the end of 2015.

Create Cultural Districts

For years, as in most other growing US metropolitan areas, the availability of space in Seattle for artists to create and to present their work has been shrinking. This reduction has taken place in direct proportion to the increased renovation of once-derelict buildings into high-rent office and retail space. The Washington Shoe Building and 619 Western building in the Pioneer Square neighborhood, where the nation's first regularly scheduled formal art walk was invented, were both lost to gentrification. Over two hundred working artists were displaced, most either moving to neighborhoods on the edge of the city or out of it entirely, seeking less expensive work spaces.

As the exodus of artists from the Pioneer Square neighborhood grew, another inner-city area of artistic activity, Capitol Hill, also began experiencing exploding land values, displacing residents and businesses. I started receiving ever more e-mails complaining of this trend. Capitol Hill's premiere longtime artists' hub, Oddfellows Hall, as with the Shoe and the 619 Western building, was slated for redevelopment. Of the roughly forty arts organizations renting space in the building, only two remained after its sale to a new owner. One was forced to move a few blocks away after receiving a 300 percent rent increase.

Although artists, shop owners, and residents met frequently and informally in the many coffee shops that dot Capitol Hill, there was little organized opposition to developers transforming their community. Someone needed to give that informal activity form and purpose. It didn't have to be someone with all the answers, just someone who was asking questions and bringing people together to find answers.

Matthew Kwatinetz, a Seattle artist and entrepreneur, decided to start those discussions. From operating a performance arts center on Capitol Hill, he was familiar with the real estate market and knew many of the artists personally. Kwatinetz provided a space to hold community forums at his business, the Capitol Hill Arts Center. He encouraged those in attendance to begin formulating a plan that could lead to retaining affordable arts spaces in the neighborhood.

An underlying theme of their meetings began to emerge: they were a united community wanting some control over their neighborhood. Once they passed that cognitive threshold, they realized that city officials needed to hear from them. I was invited to one of the forums, where more than two hundred people jammed into the meeting room that night to voice concern and outrage. The size of the turnout and the level of anger took me aback. After listening to them, I invited those present to hold a larger gathering at City Hall so the other councilmembers could hear their stories.

If you are going to hold a community gathering, invite politicians to attend so they are immersed in the physical environs of that community. The residents are also likely to feel more empowered since it is on their home turf. Holding an evening meeting with available parking and tossing in a few nibbles will ensure a good turnout. Be prepared to suggest a next step at the end of the meeting. One of the more effective ones would be to ask a councilmember to hold another forum at City Hall, and notify the media in advance. The point of the City Hall gathering is to get more councilmembers to appear and to demonstrate to the media that this is a hot topic that they should be covering. Have people with personal stories of being displaced ready to testify and to talk one-on-one with reporters.

The councilmembers who attended the City Hall gathering all came away moved and committed to doing something about the situation. But the discussion did not die there. Arts activists kept the momentum going. They suggested that the council create a citizens' advisory group with city staff assigned to it in order to make a report to the council on the nature of the problem and possible solutions. That is exactly what happened.

The arts activists worked with Councilmember Sally Clark and me to create a Cultural Overlay District Advisory Committee (CODAC) in 2008 to organize a course of action by the City. After it met for nine months it presented its recommendations to the council; one of the top recommendations was to create arts and cultural districts, which the City adopted by resolution. Following this resolution, the City conducted additional research and surveys and held more forums and community events. The City also hired staff to assist displaced artists in finding affordable work spaces.

Although there was never any direct opposition to establishing the districts, the first and second mayor during this extended period of study did not direct the City's various departments to actually establish any districts. Finally, after persistent lobbying by the community and the election of a sympathetic new mayor, Ed Murray, legislation was passed naming Capitol Hill as the city's first arts and cultural district and instituting guidelines for establishing arts districts in other neighborhoods that foster and preserve art spaces.

The market economy will continue to dominate the shape of development in Seattle, but through community organizing, citizens persuaded politicians that the public sector must intervene to protect quality of life and preserve affordable work spaces so that our city can continue to attract creative talent. It's a policy that any city government could adopt if it wishes to nourish and draw in those who are, as Richard Florida would describe them, part of the creative class.

CHAPTER 11
TAKE THE POWER AND USE IT

Homeless Encampments: The Poor Take Control

Societies have two kinds of power: people power and institutional power. In a representative democratic government, these two powers are balanced through a transparent application of laws. But when political or economic power becomes concentrated in too few hands, then you need to acquire power to realign the balance.

One approach is for a group to create a parallel power structure without receiving approval from a higher established institution. The parallel power structure not only assumes power but also acts as a legitimate authority for carrying out its functions.

The proliferation of self-managed homeless encampments, often in some of our wealthiest cities, like Seattle and Portland in the Northwest, is an example. Here individuals create their own self-governed communities because they have no other way to find secure shelter for the night.

The development of Seattle's encampments illustrates what tactics have been used to secure land and political support for their existence until affordable housing for their inhabitants once again becomes available. Scott Morrow has been working with homeless people organizing tent encampments since 1990, with the longest continuing one, Tent City 3, dating back to March 31, 2000. Previously, Morrow had been working with the Tenants Union of Washington State and was moved by seeing renters being tossed out of their homes and becoming homeless. Over time he began to see that people who found themselves homeless had different tactics and goals than the housing activists. While the activists were focused on longer-term goals like finding apartments or building new ones to provide permanent housing, those living on the streets were most concerned about where to find a safe shelter for that night.

Morrow began meeting once a week with a dozen people who were homeless to better understand their needs. At their first meeting they sought to protect themselves from being displaced during the Goodwill Games that were being held in Seattle in 1990. The Games were highlighting the competition's role in fostering good Soviet-US relations. But a possible unintended consequence might have been removing homeless people from their makeshift shelters in vacant lots and alleys. The City responded by allowing homeless encampments to use Myrtle Edwards Park during the day while the Games were going on.

With Morrow's assistance, the original group of homeless people he had met with formed the Seattle Housing and Resource Effort (SHARE), and in preparation for the winter season they tried to rent a warehouse to provide them with twenty-four-hour shelter seven days a week. Unable to find one, they decided to erect a tent encampment when they found that inexpensive military tents could be acquired at auctions. Keep in mind that tent encampments were not the first choice. The occupants would have preferred to find indoor shelter, but having been rejected by private property owners, they had no other choice.

They found an empty lot owned by Barry Ackerley, who also owned the Sonics professional basketball team. They dropped him a note asking to negotiate an arrangement, but he didn't respond. After they camped out for two weeks, newly elected mayor Norm Rice intervened and offered them a bus barn in the Lower Queen Anne neighborhood, where the Bill and Melinda Gates Foundation is now located. SHARE accepted the offer under the condition that they could manage their own shelter.

To his credit, Rice trusted that homeless people could responsibly do so and limited the barn's occupancy to one hundred people, while making sure they had access to hot water and bathroom facilities. SHARE, recognizing that there is strength through a united community, initially turned down the offer because their two-week tent encampment at Ackerley's site had attracted 152 people. They did not want to leave anyone outside. The City acknowledged that need and arranged to make available a hall in the Assumption Catholic Church just at night, meanwhile keeping the bus barn open 24/7.

The Queen Anne neighborhood's response to the encampment was divided. Their chamber received a promise from the mayor to close it down after winter. However, the neighborhood advisory group created by the City to work with the shelter people voted to let SHARE to stay. The encampment built goodwill by having transparent operations and issuing reports when people in the shelter broke their encampment code of conduct, which required sobriety, no violence, no loitering, and respecting neighbors. Most importantly, any members who broke the code could be and often were expelled from the camp by a vote by those in the encampment. In other words, discipline was self-imposed in a democratic manner.

Despite having the support of the advisory group, SHARE left the Queen Anne site when the mayor asked them to. Confrontations with the police would not have served SHARE well. They wanted the public to understand that they were cooperative and respectful of others but still committed to establishing homeless encampments. Their willingness to move from any site when requested has built goodwill with the broader public. Consequently they have continued to move around the city, most often to church properties where they have been invited to stay for a limited period of time.

One of the elements contributing to their cohesiveness is having paid staff and resident leaders. The staff get paid minimum wage, and the resident leaders are people who have lived at the camp long enough to have a knowledge of the history of what has worked for the organization, like the need to have rules to keep order. Even with 75 percent of the residents being there less than a year, the people staying in a well-managed tent encampment can develop a strong sense of purpose and community.

Richard LeMieux aptly described that sense of helping one another in an op-ed in the *Seattle Times*. He had fallen into depression after he lost everything in a major business failure: his waterfront home, possessions, friends, spouse, and family. For three years he was homeless, living on the streets or in his van. Then he found a self-managed tent encampment and saw it as a place "where miracles can happen, through mutual kindness and compassion. It can be a place where local neighbors can visit and learn that the homeless are no different from themselves—other than not having a warm, permanent place to call 'home.'" This is a condition that isn't created by an outside nonprofit agency imposing order; it grows from the working relationships that develop within a self-help community.

Encampments are not the solution to homelessness, however. From 2011 to 2014, the number of unsheltered people sleeping outside in Seattle went from just over 1,700 to more than 2,300. And that was not including roughly 6,000 people who were in area emergency shelters and transitional housing programs. As in other large cities, small clusters of homeless people, mostly men, take refuge in greenbelts or under bridges; most of these are informal, temporary arrangements without enforceable rules.

Seattle's three self-managed encampments stand out from the rest in their adherence to orderly conduct and safety. In 2015 the largest one—with the previously adopted name Nickelsville after former mayor Greg Nickels, which was not meant as nor seen as an honor—had 130 people. The other two were smaller; one had ninety-five residents, and the other had forty. All three camps, like others run by SHARE before them, had security workers on duty twenty-four hours a day and litter patrols outside the camp on a daily basis. The camps also provided bus tickets for residents to get to work or appointments. There was a food-preparation area, and volunteers often brought hot meals in the evening. No public funds had been spent for maintaining any of Seattle's encampments until the city council authorized funds to be spent to provide some minimum basic services in 2015.

Two different mayors convened citizen task forces to review the homeless situation and make recommendations. Both groups concluded that homeless encampments were useful and should be accommodated. The council came close to acting but retreated when neighborhoods opposed permanent encampments. The council passed legislation in April of 2015 with the mayor's support, designating city land for up to three encampments with a maximum of a hundred residents each.

The camps would be subject to a code of conduct similar to what was being enforced by SHARE. The council subsequently received a list of possible sites from the mayor for making the final selection so that the camps could be operational before the end of the year.

Sharon Lee, the executive director of the Low Income Housing Institute (LIHI), has been working with SHARE for over twenty years. She described self-managed encampments as "a safe 24/7 environment for people, offering stability and a good crises response solution. Caseworkers often have better access to the people who are homeless at encampments than overnight shelters."

In creating a power structure parallel to the outside world, self-managed encampments provide their residents with an opportunity to learn how to handle donations and public relations. They take personal responsibility for and have ownership over their environment. Lee concluded that "when people have a sense of ownership, they gain confidence and they hold each other accountable. They need not just physical stability but also social responsibility." In other words, they are becoming citizens.

Community Land Trusts: Housing Is Not a Commodity

Creating a power structure parallel to the existing market economy can work, but it takes patience and a willingness to work with a wide assortment of other groups. The example of Seattle's successful Homestead Community Land Trust (HCLT) shows how economic power can be shifted to a broader base of citizens by not treating housing as a commodity subject to speculation and swings in value.

Land trusts started forming to fight foreclosures and poverty, but it took decades before they became noticeably successful. Seattle's HCLT was formed by local community activists in the late eighties who wanted to gain more community control over housing resources in the Central Area and Rainier Valley. They wanted to provide affordable housing as a way to combat displacement of poor people and people of color from their neighborhoods. Activists in other cities also began forming community land trusts, and by 2004 nearly 120 community land trusts existed in thirty states, but not all of them were residential.

Generally, a community land trust owns the land and real estate, and leases it to an occupant, who receives a slight percentage of the appreciated value of the property if they move on. Sheldon Cooper, the executive director of HCLT for fifteen years, explained how the deal works. Homestead gives modest-income buyers who are priced out of Seattle's housing market the opportunity to buy a home at 30 percent to 50 percent below market value. In exchange, they agree to pass along the deal they got to the next income-eligible buyer when they sell.

The HCLT homeowner makes a steady and predictable amount of equity but does not have the opportunity to make a windfall profit if the market goes wild. They are also insulated from loss in declining markets. In addition to explaining the equity restriction, Homestead tells buyers how the land trust provides a safer form of ownership with a lower foreclosure rate, predictable equity growth, and built-in ongoing homeowner support.

Cooper's involvement with HCLT began in 1998, when he and a half dozen friends obtained an old vacant apartment building that they renovated to live in as an intentional community called the Beacon Hill House. "We wanted an ownership structure for the property that would permanently remove it from the speculative market. We saw the HCLT's mission as an opportunity to catalyze new excitement and energy," Cooper explained. Their principles:

- Housing is a human right.
- Housing is tied too closely with the success of our communities to be treated as a commodity.
- The market cannot be relied upon to provide adequate housing for low- and moderate-income households.
- The public and private investment that creates affordable housing should be long lasting, and the homes themselves should be permanently affordable.

- Investment in communities without displacing lower-income people is possible and is a matter of social justice.

By 1998, the high-tech boom was causing property values and rents to rise dramatically all over Seattle. Well-paid tech workers began working in Beacon Hill, an affordable, very racially diverse neighborhood that is close to downtown and has great vistas. As gentrification began, HCLT decided they wanted to purchase houses to allow low-income residents to remain in their neighborhood.

There was a problem, however; HCLT had been dormant for a number of years after the first house it tried to secure fell through due to lack of financing. So Cooper and others had to set about revitalizing it. Their first meeting was an open house to show off a property that could be donated to HCLT. There was general excitement and support for this second attempt, with almost fifty people attending.

In a break from past efforts, they invited allies, like the Tenants Union, Seattle Displacement Coalition, and the LIHI, to attend rather than the general public, because they were looking for people who wanted to actively support their effort. That was a smart move. To build an organization, you need committed volunteers and allied organizations who will offer staff or monetary support. Opening up your first meeting to the public without those resources might lead the organization to failure.

Those allies helped HCLT overcome its first major obstacle, lack of funds. They managed to launch operations by securing a $2,500 grant from LIHI and some Department of Housing and Urban Planning technical assistance funds from the Institute for Community Economics (ICE). Homestead's board hired Cooper as a part-time director, and he hired an AmeriCorps VISTA volunteer to keep their expenses low. Then they identified their project, which was a single-family house in a low-income neighborhood.

They borrowed additional funds from a community-development finance institute, Impact Capital, and got grants from the City of Seattle and Washington State. They partnered with the nonprofit YouthBuild for some of the construction, solicited donations from local construction companies, and held many community work parties. The key to their success in obtaining this home and later many others was that they were willing to partner with other organizations but still kept true to their principles. Achieving a balance between working with government agencies or private lenders and keeping to your organizational goals can be challenging. If those goals are compromised, the very purpose of the organization comes into question.

However, besides tight funding, Homestead faced skepticism and even hostility. Some housing advocates believed that public resources should be targeted exclusively at helping people who were homeless, while some real estate agents objected to limiting the market value of a house in a land trust.

Some of the city staff preferred providing low-income people with affordable loans to help them buy market-rate homes, arguing that the market appreciation of value in their homes should be entirely theirs to keep. These were all current practices that had not resulted in any permanent low-income housing, because all of the housing eventually returned to the marketplace. The very concept of the land trust was to remove the housing from the marketplace. It was a radical concept for many low-income housing advocates, because they could not conceive of creating long-term affordability for owned housing.

Cooper and others in the community land trust movement could have given up and agreed that perhaps their dream was impractical. But instead they engaged these concerns through dialogue and consistently pointing out the benefits of their approach.

It is important when facing opposition to a new concept or a new approach to an ongoing problem that you have two things: patience to talk through others' concerns and examples that show this concept or approach has been tried elsewhere. In this instance, Cooper was able to point to the Burlington Community Land Trust (BCLT) in Vermont. It was and still is the nation's largest land trust, with more than 2,500 members involved in a democratic stewardship of land to provide permanent homes. It was the first municipally funded community land trust, but others have followed.

Without compromising their principles, HCLT partnered with one of the other nonprofit housing providers so that its homes became part of the land trust and were subject to long-term affordability restrictions. Having lived in a land trust residential property for twenty-five years, I recognized their value and asked city staff and a citizens' advisory committee to use funding from the City's low-income-housing levy to incentivize land trusts. Prior to this change neither the City nor the State funded agencies or developers to provide permanent affordability in housing ownership.

This change in policy did not happen overnight. It took six years for Cooper to purchase the first home under his direction. As he said, "We were very small, underresourced, and fighting to establish Homestead as a real housing solution in Seattle. Even though it was hard, I never considered giving up." That was due in part to having a supportive community, which is critical in any major effort to change the status quo. A group of twenty to thirty land trust advocates and practitioners made it a priority to meet face to face in the Northwest for two days twice a year for well over a decade. They shared stories, problem solved, and dreamed together.

But their dreams were tied to a solid strategy of starting small and making something tangible happen. Homestead identified a single-home project and managed to secure the resources to bring it into the trust. It took twenty-two months of Homestead's entire focus and resulted in one home. But it was a real, tangible start. "It introduced many people and partners to the concept and created a real win at the end," Cooper explained. Ten years after securing that home, they had 150 homes, and their goal is to be adding a hundred homes to the land trust per year by 2020.

Luckily, others who share Cooper's ambition do not have to start from scratch; the National Community Land Trust Network provides research, advocacy, education, and support for those wishing to provide permanently affordable land, homes, and community assets.

If citizens want to gain control over their housing market through land trusts, they need a clear objective of what they wish to achieve. They need to make allies with those nonprofit developers already in the housing field and with their local government leaders in order to obtain low-interest start-up loans or outright grants, as was done in Seattle. Although initially skeptical, the City has come to see how this alternative approach to obtaining affordable housing is productive, and public support has continued to grow.

Student Power

Nourishing a vibrant democracy calls for an educated citizenry, and that opportunity begins in high schools and colleges. While a number of states require some type of civics requirement in school curriculums, too often it is limited to reviewing a state's history. At the college level, when students become eligible to vote, civics is largely ignored as a basic requirement. Unfortunately the emphasis on training students for jobs has overshadowed the need for colleges to educate students about their responsibilities, duties, and rights as citizens.

There are two ways that students can accomplish this. The first would be through greater student participation in their college's governance and in the selection of their curriculums. The second is by voting in local elections.

Student participation at a university happens largely through involvement in the governance structure. There is almost always a student government, and depending on the university, that body may have control over a portion of the student fees reserved for student-related activities. If those funds are not constrained, use them to hold forums on campus that highlight student needs. One of the most obvious issues may be tuition cost. Nationally the burden of student debt approached a trillion dollars in 2011, surpassing both credit card and auto-loan debt. The average student graduating from a four-year institution in the United States that year owed more than $25,000 in student loans. Certainly, it would be a worthy event to spend student fees on.

Most importantly, have a student representative on the real decision-making body, the board of trustees. A 2010 AGB (Association of Governing Boards of Universities and Colleges) study showed that more than 70 percent of public institution boards include one or more students. Due largely to state laws, half of public institutions have voting student board members. Sarah Elfreth's *The Young Guardians: Students as Stewards of the Past, Present, and Future of American Higher Education* provides details about how students are named to the boards of public institutions. Meanwhile, only 21 percent of private colleges and universities have at least one student member on their governing board, and less than 9 percent of student trustees have a vote.

Having the student representative on the trustee board be a delegate from the student government raises the value of that body and allows it to influence the university's budget and administrative rules. Students should help shape their universities, much like citizens help shape their cities. They should have a voice about how their money is being spent. For instance, a number of universities and colleges have devoted less money to educational curriculums and more to funding sports teams or constructing buildings like food courts, spa-like athletic facilities, and elaborate performing arts centers that don't provide more classrooms.

Having greater student participation may also halt the tendency for educational institutions to be run more like corporations; private institutions emphasize greater profits, and public ones emphasize activities that can attract corporate or other wealthy donors. This corporate orientation has also led to an ever-higher percentage of the faculty being adjunct professors, who are often paid a fraction of what tenured professors receive and lack sufficient office space and administrative help. And finally, they do not have the job security that tenure would bring. The American Association of University Professors reports that in just three decades the percentage of adjuncts has gone from 43 percent of professors to nearly 70 percent of professors at all colleges and universities. Students suffer from this trend. Several studies have determined that freshmen taught by many part-timers are more likely to drop out.

Student power can and should be exercised outside the campus as well. By voting in elections, students can change state laws. For instance, their votes could go to candidates who would require state institutions to have a higher percentage of full-time professors, to spend a minimum amount of total funds on educational purposes, and to allow staff and faculty to collectively bargain for benefits.

Those with more education are also more likely to vote. A poll conducted by the Center for Information and Research on Civic Learning and Engagement showed that college-educated youth are twice as likely to vote in an election as those without a college education. Also, registering students to vote at their college addresses increases their participation in elections; their turnout is 8 to 10 percent higher than those registered under their parents' address.

Youth (those eighteen to twenty-nine years old) have consistently voted along a more progressive line, voting for more Democrats than Republicans. This was most evident in President Barack Obama's first campaign for presidency in 2008, which saw students voting in greater numbers than in previous decades. And that was an increase over a significant turnout in 2004, when 20.1 million voters were eighteen to twenty-nine years old, rivaling the 22.3 million voters over sixty-five years of age.

The youth vote is a large voting block with tremendous potential to influence elections. In 2012, 46 million were eligible to vote, while 39 million seniors were eligible to vote. Since many young voters are new voters, the ones who register are more likely to vote than the average registered voter: in 2004, 81.6 percent of newly registered voters went to the polls. That rate was even higher for young registered voters in 2008, when 84 percent of them cast a ballot.

Conservatives have passed restrictive rules that make it harder for students to register and vote at their colleges. A number of these laws force students to provide identification and meet residential requirements that exceed federal laws. Proponents of these laws argue that these steps are necessary to avoid fraudulent voting. However, a five-year investigation by President George W. Bush's Department of Justice noted that out of millions of student votes cast, there were only eighty-six convictions of improper voting.

The Fair Elections Legal Network, formed in 2006, has a staff of attorneys and advocates working to eliminate barriers to voting by improving the administration of elections for students and minorities. Unions have a long tradition of encouraging voter registration, and the AFL-CIO's voter rights protection project, formed in 2008, took their efforts one step further by providing election-related materials for schools that list key deadlines and polling locations.

The Student Public Interest Research Groups (PIRGs) established the New Voters Project, which increased student voter turnout in the November 2012 election over the 2008 election. For the 2014 elections the Student PIRGs organized a nonpartisan youth voter mobilization campaign to reach a hundred college campuses in twelve states.

The nonpartisan Campus Election Engagement Project is a classic example of the power of an individual to effect change. Author and public speaker Paul Loeb personally raised funds to initiate the project, which worked with 500 campuses in 2008 and 750 campuses in 2012, helping schools to increase student involvement in elections by using the project's campus election checklist and organizing guide. The project has increased student voter turnout in most of the states where it has been used.

Every generation of students has the power to shape the future. Some forty years after the sixties, a poll taken by Morley Winograd and Michael Hais showed that 70 percent of freshman students believe that it is "essential or very important to help people in need." And in that same poll, 25 percent of students say they have demonstrated for a cause.

Being a student is a temporary status, while being a citizen is a lifetime one. Education at every level must allow students to openly express their opinions and shape their political environment in order to prepare for citizenship. As Justice Louis D. Brandeis wrote in 1927, "the greatest menace to freedom is an inert people." Citizen vigilance for sustaining a just and responsive democracy begins with students organizing and voting.

Democracy Dies without You

Democracy only works when all citizens can fairly participate in it. Otherwise, it is a sham, regardless if it is a people's democracy, a God-ordained democracy, or a representative democracy. In the most definitive sense, a real democracy allows its people to vote with unfettered access to both information and the ballot. Without meeting those two basic conditions, even well-intentioned efforts will lead to the ossification of government and the eventual growth of a privileged class.

Individuals are also obligated to sustain a vibrant, responsive democracy. Individuals must make the effort to educate themselves about candidates and issues. They must also understand that democracies are not revolutions. They move slowly. But the direction they move in can be determined democratically. To ignore this is to become cynical and feel powerless. And that becomes true as more citizens withdraw, leaving power in fewer hands.

Federal, state, or local governments can either hinder or assist the democratic process. Many of the ways to improve citizen access to the ballot rely on cooperation among all three levels of government. However, municipal government can initiate ways to increase voter turnout. This is important, because local election turnouts lag behind state and federal races. And the gap is growing. University of Wisconsin research collected over the last decade in 144 large US cities showed a decline in voter turnout in odd-numbered years, when local elections are held, going from 26.6 percent in 2001 to 21 percent in 2011. *Governing* magazine reviewed the report and concluded that there is a long-term trend of waning voter participation in larger cities, which typically have diverse ethnic populations. This trend has skewed the voting public toward a nonurban population that tends to be white, more affluent, and older. As one might expect, a University of California, San Diego, professor found that low-turnout elections contribute to uneven prioritization of public spending, often to the detriment of minorities.

Since data on voter turnout is more readily available by state than by cities, I'll list three methods that the six states with the highest rates of voter participation have employed to attain their higher level of citizen involvement.

The top three states in voter turnout all mention same-day registration as being the most significant factor. The option of mailing in ballots is identified most frequently among the top six states. As of 2014, Washington and Oregon were the only two states that have switched entirely to mailed-in ballots, and both have higher participation rates than the national average. In Seattle, an all mail-in election has led our local elections to regularly post a turnout of over 40 percent. For comparison, Los Angeles' highly contested mayoral election in 2013 saw just over 20 percent of registered voters cast their ballots.

Likewise, in New York's mayoral election of Bill de Blasio, the turnout of 26 percent was the lowest since the 1950s.

Two other strategies have increased voter participation on both the state and local levels. The first is to provide a greater choice of candidates. Public funding of campaigns accomplishes this, because candidates are not dependent on soliciting large donors. Public funding has resulted in more women candidates and an overall greater diversity of candidates, both in terms of demographic profiles and politics. The greater the selection of candidates, the more likely that people will vote.

The second way to increase voter participation is to bring important public-spending issues up for a vote. The conservatives have used this method nationally in many states and localities since 1978, when California passed Proposition 13, which capped the state real estate tax on property to 1 percent of its assessed value. It was widely popular, receiving almost 65 percent of the vote and bringing nearly 70 percent of registered voters to the polls. The downside was that California's university system sank in its national standing from the top to the bottom of the barrel due to lack of funding. In Seattle, we took this antitax approach and applied it to the issue of publicly funding sport arenas for private professional teams. If there was public funding, the taxpayers had to be paid back with an interest rate fixed to treasury bonds. It passed with over 70 percent of the vote.

Despite political differences between conservatives and liberals, or right-wing and left-wing activists, the glue that holds all of us within the sphere of a democracy is the belief that we make our laws through elected representation. A Seattle police officer who attacked city government for violating his liberty by requiring him to attend social justice training classes wrote, "elections have consequences." Eric Davis, a cousin of Michael Brown, who was an unarmed youth killed by a police officer in Ferguson, Missouri, under highly questionable circumstances, said, "Show up at the voting booths. Let your voices be heard." Both of them understood where the power for changing the world lies—it's with you.

A READING LIST

These books helped frame the stories, strategies, and advice that have influenced my life and *Becoming a Citizen Activist*. Each of us takes away lessons from them according to what we see. None have the answer; that is for each of us to figure out.

Alexander, Michelle. *The New Jim Crow: Mass Incarceration in the Age of Colorblindness*. New York: New Press, 2010.

Alinsky, Sauld. *Rules for Radicals: A Pragmatic Primer for Realistic Radicals*. New York: Vintage, 1989.

Armey, Dick & Matt Kibbe. *Give Us Liberty: A Tea Party Manifesto*. New York: HarperCollins, 2010.

Atkins, Gary L. *Gay Seattle: Stories of Exile and Belonging*. Seattle: University of Washington Press, 2003.

Harrington, Michael. *The Other America: Poverty in the United States*. New York: Macmillan, 1962.

Hayden, Tom et al. *The Port Huron Statement*. New York: Students for a Democratic Society, 1962.

Jones, Van. *Rebuild the Dream*. New York: Nation Books, 2012.

Kennedy, John F. *Profiles in Courage*. New York: Pocket Books, 1957.

Loeb, Paul Rogat. *Soul of a Citizen: Living with Conviction in Challenging Times*. 2nd ed. New York: St. Martin's Griffin, 2010.

McPeak, Vivian. *Protestival: Seattle Hempfest; a 20-Year Retrospective*. Austin: AH HA Publishing, 2011.

Mills, C. Wright. *The Power Elite*. New York: Oxford University Press, 1956.

Sale, Kirkpatrick. *SDS*. New York: Random House, 1973.

Sanders, Jeffrey Craig. *Seattle & the Roots of Urban Sustainability: Inventing Ecotopia*. Pittsburgh: University of Pittsburg Press, 2010.

Reich, Michael, Ken Jacobs, Miranda Dietz, eds. *When Mandates Work: Raising Labor Standards at the Local Level*. Edited by Berkeley: University of California Press, 2014.

ABOUT THE AUTHOR

NICK LICATA is from a working-class family where neither parent graduated from high school. Licata, who couldn't read until the age of nine, was the first of his relatives to attend college. He led the local chapter of Students for a Democratic Society (SDS) at Bowling Green State University and subsequently was elected student body president. He became a Seattle city councilmember despite being significantly outspent and the majority of the council, the mayor, and both daily newspapers supporting his opponent. Elected to five terms, in 2012 he was named by the *Nation* as Progressive Municipal Official of the Year and twice named Best Local Politician by the *Seattle Weekly*. In 2003, Licata authored the children's novel *Princess Bianca and the Vandals*.

Visit **BecomingaCitizenActivist.org** to share your stories, strategies, and advice on how to make our democracy accountable to our citizens.